Is It I, Lord?

ALSO BY JAMES O. CHATHAM

Enacting the Word: Using Drama in Preaching
(Westminster John Knox Press)

Is It I, Lord?
Discerning God's Call to Be a Pastor

James O. Chatham

Westminster John Knox Press
LOUISVILLE • LONDON

Scripture quotations, unless otherwise indicated, are from the New Revised Standard Version of the Bible, copyright © 1989 by the Division of Christian Education of the National Council of the Churches of Christ in the U.S.A. and are used by permission.

Scripture quotations marked RSV are from the Revised Standard Version of the Bible, are copyright © 1946, 1952, 1971, and 1973 by the Division of Christian Education of the National Council of the Churches of Christ in the U.S.A., and are used by permission.

Book design by Sharon Adams
Cover design by Night & Day Design

Published by Westminster John Knox Press
Louisville, Kentucky

This book is printed on acid-free paper that meets the American National Standards Institute Z39.48 standard. ♾

PRINTED IN THE UNITED STATES OF AMERICA

02 03 04 05 06 07 08 09 10 11 — 10 9 8 7 6 5 4 3 2 1

Library of Congress Cataloging-in-Publication Data

Chatham, James O., 1937–
    Is It I, Lord?: discerning God's call to be a pastor /
    by James O. Chatham; TK.
      p. cm.
    ISBN 0-664-22672-8 (alk. paper)
      1. Clergy—Appointment, call, and election. I. Title

BV4011.4.C47 2002
253'.2—dc21   2002071309

IN MEMORY OF
HARRY G. GOODYKOONTZ
AND
IN HONOR OF
BETTY L. GOODYKOONTZ,
MY IN-LAWS,
TWO LIVES LIVED IN ANSWER
TO GOD'S CALL

Contents

Chapter 1

Is God Calling You to Be a Pastor?

*I*s God calling you to be a pastor? This book is designed to ask that question with you.

God called Abraham and Sarah to leave their home, their family, their identity, and sojourn in an unfamiliar land.

God called Moses to lead Israel out of Egypt.

God called Rahab to shelter undercover agents sent to Jericho.

God called Deborah to rid Israel of the yoke of King Jabin of Canaan.

God called Samuel to anoint Israel's first king.

God called Ruth, a Moabite, to join the lineage of David.

God called Nathan to speak both promise and judgment to King David.

God called Amos to declare that God was far, far bigger than Israel's religious certainties.

God called Isaiah to summon the people of Israel to open their prosperity-glazed eyes and see God in their midst.

God called Jeremiah to speak hard, difficult words about Israel's future.

God called Elizabeth in her old age to become the mother of a prophet.

God called Mary to give birth to God incarnate.

God called Simon and Andrew, James and John, to leave their fishing boats and follow Jesus.

God called Levi to give up tax collecting and become a disciple.

God called Saul, a devout religious believer, to put on new eyes and see God, Jesus, and humanity in a radically different way.

God called Lydia, a cloth merchant, to host the first church in Philippi.

From the beginning, *God has called people;* God has stepped into their lives and pointed them in new directions. God does this throughout the Bible; few pages go by without it. Is this not a strong signal that *God is going to call us too*; that in some moment when we are involved in a normal day's pursuits, God will walk up the lake shore and beckon us to leave our fishing boats for a future we had not planned?

"Follow me," Jesus said to Simon and Andrew (Mark 1:17).

"Go from your country and your kindred and your father's house to the land that I will show you," God said to Abraham and Sarah (Gen. 12:1).

Turn from your present and take up My future. Abandon the securities and venture into insecurity. Depart from the world you know into a world I alone know.

The path of answering God's call is not easy. God does not build a straight highway through the desert to guarantee safe passage. There are sharp turns and difficult barriers, rules to satisfy, procedures to follow, small personalities to tolerate, big egos to survive, tests to pass, put-downs to ignore, discouragements to forget, failures to overcome. The journey of answering God's call is hard! No one should ever think otherwise.

At times, the call will be clear and compelling, certain as a familiar voice. At other times, it will be distant and faint, little more that a vague memory.

But if the Bible says anything clearly, it says this: God calls us. Calls us to do whatever God has in mind. Calls us to set a great many other things aside and follow God's bidding. Is God calling you to be a pastor?

I have been a pastor for more than thirty-five years. A lot has changed in that time. Churches, sermons, worship, music, spirituality, pastoral leadership, church expectations of a pastor—they all are different.

But the basics have not changed. We are to perform the same essential roles we always did, but in new ways. Those essential roles are what I want to discuss in this book. I want to tell you how you will spend your vocational life if you decide to become a pastor. It is easy to glamorize the picture, to emit sentimental puff. Many people seem to think that being a pastor is a highly rewarding career that trades the cares of this world for profound spiritual gratification, a perpetual high with God. That is romantic schlock. My intention is to cut through the mystique.

I approach the task with considerable caution. Who am I, who is anyone, to guide another person concerning God's call? It is God who calls, not I. God takes the people we are—our considerable strengths and our troubling weaknesses, our apparent confidence and our hidden uncertainties—and works through us. It is a miracle far greater than anything I can understand. God is well known across the Bible for selecting people I never would have picked—migrant laborers, murderers, prostitutes, whorehouse operators, old women, teenage girls, fishermen, tax collectors, and religious zealots. In my class in seminary were a meteorologist, a bank teller, a professional football player, a bartender, and a used car salesman. God calls the people God wants, and I tread humbly on God's ground.

But still, there are some things to be said. There are some people who strongly should consider becoming pastors, and others who probably should not. There has to be a gate, and humans have to tend it. The gate should not be narrow, but neither should people be encouraged to follow any voice they hear without consulting a larger wisdom.

Be warned: I have loved being a pastor! I speak with strong positive bias—not a bias toward the answer you should give, but toward the answer I gave. Certainly there have been negatives, lots of them. I will tell you some and ask you to think about them carefully. But, overall, I will encourage you.

I hear stories about how some congregations torture their pastors, criticizing them viciously for things they say, expecting them to be people they are not, requiring them, and often their spouses, to be property owned by the congregation. There are bits of this in my experience, but not much. I will speak as one whose life has been rich and full because of the calling.

In chapter 2, I tell you the story of my call. It won't be like yours, but it's a place to start. I will also tell you of several other people from diverse backgrounds who responded to God's call. My hope is that you can get a larger perspective on who and where you are.

In chapters 3–6, I will state as clearly as I can the essence of the pastoral vocation, the fundamental pursuits of the work.

A pastor needs to have multiple talents: To be a theologian, constantly honing and shaping his or her insights about God. To be a fairly decent biblical scholar who keeps up with the academic field. To be well informed, reading the morning newspaper and scanning the sociology/anthropology section in the local bookstore regularly. To be able to write well. To speak acceptably and interestingly in public (this is often underestimated). To know at least a bit about music. To be an effective organizational planner. To be able to raise money. To understand finance. To be a good listener and counselor. To care genuinely about people. And, when the pastor finally has to admit that he or she can't do all these things, the pastor needs to be able to find others who can.

I have spent my professional life distilling from this array the blue chip items. In chapters 3–6, I will tell you what I think they are.

Chapter 3 will talk about our most basic task—identifying the Holy One in our midst.

Chapter 4 will discuss believing in and proclaiming the miracle of resurrection.

Chapter 5 will deal with guiding people and communities in finding direction.

Chapter 6 will speak of the sacred privilege we enjoy in having nearly an open invitation to enter into people's lives.

In chapter 7, I want to discuss words, speech—the pastor's main tool. I want to show you how words are the most powerful and creative force in the universe.

In chapter 8, I will make the point that a pastor needs to be a person of conviction, someone who believes in something strongly enough that it motivates him or her in an exceptional way.

In chapter 9, we will look at the self-critical element that needs to underlie every plan we make, every cause we champion, every worship we lead, every message we preach.

Chapter 10 will be my sermon to you about what I call "God's partiality," a picture of the God I find in the Bible and what it means for pastoral leadership.

In chapter 11, I will use the call story of Moses from Exodus 3 to depict the resistances you and I put up in responding to God's call.

Chapter 12 will be my checklist, a collection of dos and don'ts as you make your decision on becoming a pastor.

Chapter 13 will describe a bit of what seminary is like and tell several stories from my seminary experience.

Chapter 14 will conclude with the voices I suggest you listen to carefully as you evaluate your call.

Is God calling you to be a pastor? I am not the one to say. You are. But I invite you to walk with me through this exploration.

Chapter 2

How It Was for Me, and Some Others

*I*n the hope that you can compare yourself with some of your brothers and sisters, I begin by telling several call stories. The first is my own.

The initial cracks in my certainty appeared when I was in graduate school. I had decided long before that I wanted to become an electrical engineer. I had been twisting wires since I was eleven, witnessing the miracles of electromagnetic communication, and my fascination had never diminished. The hottest college graduates in the country in those post-Sputnik years were engineers. They were being gulped up ravenously by a nation seriously frightened that we had fallen behind in space technology. Industry recruiters nearly lived on campus; engineers were even more in demand than football players. I could hardly wait to become one of them.

But, as my degree came near, I found myself less sure instead of more. There were two reasons. First was the question, Did I really want to spend my life in an industrial laboratory? The work of an electrical engineer tended to be cutoff, entangled far more with circuits and gadgetry than with human beings. There was a fable that said that the happiest engineer was the one who had work instructions slid under the lab door on Monday morning, and who slid the completed work back out on Friday afternoon. Though I was not the most gregarious person on earth, I suspected I needed more human interaction than that.

But then, there was the larger reason. I had spent my college summers working for an engineering company. The task of my work team had been to perfect a small electronic box that provided timing pulses for the guidance system of the Nike Zeus intercontinental ballistic missile, the clock that regulated the entire device. I had taken pride in my work. It had required both knowledge and imagination. But I realized that I was proud of it only as long as I ignored its final purpose. The Nike Zeus was designed to kill tens of thousands of Russians. We were one small element in a very large project aimed at giving our national leaders the capacity to incinerate Moscow if they saw fit.

Was that how I wanted to spend my life? Would money—we earned lots of it—be a strong enough incentive to get me to ignore what I was actually doing?

I worked under a supervisor who was a brilliant engineer. His breadth of knowledge was inspiring, his technical insights amazing. He was also acutely paranoid. A devoted disciple of Senator Joseph McCarthy and a committed far-right-wing Christian, he believed in his heart that the U.S.S.R. was on a mission to annihilate both the United States and God. He believed that devoting his life to killing communists was the most faithful and the most patriotic thing he could do. His work was exactly right for him.

Mine wasn't. My midtwenties were making me increasingly aware that I needed to do something with my life that I fundamentally believed in, something I thought was ultimately worthwhile. That was the first major crack in my engineering certainty.

Then a strange thing happened. T. Hartley Hall IV, a campus pastor at my college, said to me rather offhandedly one day, "Chatham, when are you going to get out of this engineering stuff and do what you really ought to do with your life?"

I don't think I replied. I was stunned. I probably wasn't articulate enough to reply. But that simple comment set off fireworks in my head. T. Hartley thought I could do it. T. Hartley was no casual observer; later, he became a seminary president. He wouldn't make that comment without good reason. I had grown up around the church. I was fascinated with biblical history. I was bailing out of engineering. Should I think about it?

I prayed, listened, consulted, visited a seminary. I took tests, talked with people. And, finally, I decided to do it. There was little assurance. I still could have become an engineer. Nothing made me certain that I was doing the right thing. But I decided. After finishing the engineering degree, I would enroll in seminary.

I went home at Christmas and told my mother. She was fixing supper. "You what?" she asked. She was stunned!

My mother had been a college dropout in the Great Depression. She bore deep in her soul a strong anxiety over whether her children would grow up earning enough money to live. She had thought she had her son moving in a safe direction. Now, suddenly, she wasn't sure. Why was I changing? She was shocked.

But she got over it and became my supporter. I think she realized down deep that there was no need to do anything else.

I enrolled at Union Theological Seminary in Virginia, having essentially no idea what I was doing. I had gained an identity in my college; here, I was just another anonymous junior showing up to take baby Hebrew.

What a strange place! I became immediately aware that I was surrounded by Davidson College graduates. I had spent six years studying electromagnetic waves and differential equations at two pages per hour. They had spent their college life studying Kant and Schleiermacher and Hemingway and Faulkner at two pages per minute. And they had a very subtle way of letting you know what a superior education they had had—which they indeed had! I don't even think they knew they were doing it. But with my fragile ego, I knew. I was intimidated, wondering if this was really a place for me.

I spent the next three years (in fact, I spent the next thirty years) scrapping and scraping to catch up with those Davidson students. There was lots of history I did not know, lots of philosophy I couldn't understand, lots of literature I had never read. I remember in my first semester sitting in Old Testament Introduction and essentially not understanding a word the professor was saying about recent developments in historical-critical scholarship. I simply tried to write down everything he said, take it to the library, and see if I could make sense of it. Through my first year of seminary I was lost, having no idea whether I was doing poorly or well, just feeling my way forward through a dark unknown.

I was a senior before I finally realized that I could do theological education. Many of the Davidson folks had left by then, and the ones who remained had become considerably more humble. We were all by that time trudging side by side, trying to prop one another up and keep the light in view.

After graduation, my first job was in southwest Mississippi. I was the pastor of two Presbyterian churches—total membership: 180. Freedom Summer, 1964—Mississippi in every sense was as hot as a branding iron.

In my second week in the ministry, Herman Galbreath, one of my church members, was shot and killed by his next-door neighbor on the dirt road that adjoined their homes. It was the culmination of a disagreement that was nearly as old as I was. The next night, a seventeen-year-old boy, who had been to the funeral home for Herman's wake, turned over his father's pickup truck on a desolate road and lay unconscious in a puddle of gasoline for six hours. He died in the hospital three days later. The next day, an eighty-three-year-old man in the village died of a heart attack as he was grieving the news of the first two tragedies. My baptism included a murder, a car accident death, and a heart attack in six days. I would note many times afterward that community-wrenching events seem to happen in threes. I have no idea why.

During my first year in the ministry, I counseled repeatedly with a fifty-year-old alcoholic who was trying to reclaim his life. I also performed my first marriage, Jackie and Ken, two pleasant farm kids who, I am told, are still married and live in Jackson.

I visited a lot of people in homes, in hospitals, and on sidewalks—getting to know their strengths, their loves, their idiosyncrasies, their prejudices, their resident demons, and what was really important in their lives. I learned that the most valuable addiction a pastor can develop is *listening to people intently.*

Albert Lehmann's Ford dealership was torched by the Ku Klux Klan in retaliation for Albert's openly expressed views on race relations. At this moment, Albert is a tottering ninety-two-year-old in Port Gibson, Mississippi, still able to carry on a good conversation and still a treasured friend.

I worked on the steering committee to bring Head Start to our town. Head Start had just been initiated by the federal government, which desperately wanted the ninth poorest county in the nation to stop sending uneducated poor kids up the Mississippi River to Chicago.

I covered a lot of Jefferson County miles in the pickup truck of county agent Wilton Dykes. Wilton and I made house calls together—he to inquire about the fields and the crops, and I to talk about the family and the spirit. We made a good tandem and became close friends.

I attended negotiating meetings between the town merchants, most of whom were my church members, and civil rights leader Charles Evers, who had clamped an economic boycott on the town.

As my wife will readily testify, I preached some of the worst sermons of my life, awful stuff that would make me cringe to look at it a few years later. I kept those sermon manuscripts for two decades, but finally they were eaten by silverfish in our attic, a fitting fate. My early sermons were living proof of how forgiving both God and church members can be.

Through those months I came to realize, by way of a profound satisfaction, that the pastorate was the right place for me. The main territory of the pastor is human life, the most valuable thing on the planet. I was working now to build lives, not destroy them.

All calls are different. I want to tell you some other stories. I hope you find at least a piece of yourself in them.

Eugene. Eugene was the son of a family without much money. His mother was a Baptist, his father an agnostic who had no use for what he considered the hypocrisy of religion. Gene's family never went to church when he was young. Christian discipleship was not something he grew up knowing anything about.

As a high schooler, Gene was invited by his next-door neighbor to go to church with him. He went and found it appealing. He was baptized at age 16.

Gene found faith and the Bible very interesting and attractive. His mother and father had divorced by this time, and he needed community, which the church provided. The church, a small, very traditional congregation led by a dispensationalist pastor, encouraged him along, making him feel good about his future.

A seasoned Sunday school teacher in that congregation said to him at the end of one day's class, "Gene, you're going to teach in the church someday." She handed him her own teaching Bible as a gift, a Scofield Reference Study Bible. He treasured and read that Bible for many months afterward.

While in college, Gene became a counselor at a summer camp. The camp director, a pastor, spent numerous off-hours with Gene, discussing the pastorate and God's call.

Gene was finally convinced by a peer friend to apply to the Presbyterian Church to become a candidate for the ministry. As he approached his candidacy interview, he tried very hard to conjure up some special sign that would "prove" God's call. There was a favorite place out in the woods by a stream where Gene had gone by himself many times to relax and meditate. He went there one day and stayed for a long, long time, praying fervently that God would send him a clear signal. He would have been pleased to see a twig floating upstream in the creek—anything! Nothing happened. He came away disappointed, not to mention doubtful.

Gene appeared before the examining group with two other young men who also sought to enter the ministry. The first to speak told of his many, many relatives who had been pastors before him: his father, his grandfathers, his great-grandfathers, his uncles, his cousins—the list seemed to have no end. He was certain that God was calling him to continue the tradition of his family. The second told of heaven-rending signs that had been revealed to him, remarkable stories of visions and miracles. By the time Gene got up to speak, he was wondering if he had anything worthwhile and honest he could say. He said, simply, "I think I have been given a fairly good intellect, and I want to use it in the Lord's work." He was accepted, along with the others, as a candidate for the ministry.

Gene would finish college, finish seminary, earn a Ph.D. in biblical studies and become a seminary professor and academic dean.

Majid. Majid was a native of Pakistan. His father worked

on the maintenance staff of a theological seminary, helping keep up the grounds and offices. "There were three types of people at the seminary," Majid says, "teachers, students, and servants. My father was a servant."

The seminary professed officially that all human beings were God's valued children, that hierarchy and caste were to be rejected. But the reality was different. The seminary would hold community functions to which everyone was invited: teachers, students, workers, and their families. These meals belied the seminary's profession. "Servant's children were anything but welcome," Majid says. "It was made very clear to us that we were servant's children. We were constantly reminded that we did not belong there." It became so demeaning that Majid's family stopped attending the meals. Majid himself came to hate the seminary where his father worked, to hate Christianity. He wanted nothing to do with it. His father had to keep his job to earn a family income, but Majid grew into adolescence believing that God and Jesus and anyone associated with them were intolerant tyrants, demanding but never showing love.

When Majid was sixteen, one of his good friends was converted to Christianity by a Pentecostal evangelist. The friend began to appeal to Majid. He took Majid to his Pentecostal church and began to read the Bible with him. Majid joined the church. Even at that point, he was beginning to realize that not everything this church believed could he believe. Their thought world was far different from his. But he appreciated their friendship, liked their meetings, and joined wholeheartedly in their worship.

Over several years, Majid became an avid Bible reader. He devoured the Bible's stories and pondered the letters and prophecies. He found the Bible deeply engaging and needed no encouragement in maintaining a rigorous Bible-reading discipline. He came to understand that revealed in its pages was a God who knew him, a God who loved him.

The ultimate turning point in Majid's life came when he realized that the hatred that had consumed him was miraculously gone, that he was no longer living in bitter reaction against the past but in hopeful anticipation of the future. He had become a new person.

He soon discerned that God was also calling him, Majid, to become a pastor. Unlikely as it seemed, it was true. He possessed a keen intellect and decided to devote that intellect to God's service, even though he could have commanded a much greater income in some other profession.

Majid announced his decision to his father and mother. "No way!" was their response. "We are hoping that you will become a lawyer and change the plight of the family. By all means, you are *not* going to enroll in that seminary! In the first place, they would never let you in, and in the second, they would quickly kick you out." His parents were adamant.

However, the president of the seminary, the person most responsible for the negative attitude toward Majid's family, died shortly thereafter. Majid investigated the seminary and discovered that he could get in. He enrolled, graduated at the top of his class, and has become one of the most respected pastors in his denomination. He has completed a doctor of ministry degree in the United States and has turned down a very prestigious job to return to the 100-family congregation of which he is pastor. He has also become an adjunct faculty member of his seminary in Pakistan, teaching church history.

Ann. Ann was baptized as an infant and was part of the church from her earliest days. It was in her fifth grade Sunday school class, however, that she began to think about religion seriously. Her teachers positively made the Bible come alive for Ann, turning its characters into real people like her. Ann saw clearly the vibrant Christian faith of these two women. They told stories that showed how God was involved in people's lives. Ann felt highly valued. She understood that these two women very much wanted something for her. She was deeply touched by the relation of the two with God and with the Bible.

In junior high school, Ann encountered Barb and Sandy as youth leaders. Barb and Sandy "were literally in love with Jesus." They made a personal relationship with Jesus seem very important.

Ann took part in her church's youth group throughout high school, a very meaningful experience for her.

As she looked toward college, Ann picked a denominational university in her region. She started out as an engineering major, but her main interest, she realizes now, was in learning about the Bible. She took Bible courses along with her technical work. She switched from engineering to biology. She continued to take Bible courses. It took her, in fact, six years to get her biology degree because she overloaded herself with Bible courses. She served as student-life coordinator in her dorm, and was responsible for leading weekly Bible studies. She also became a peer adviser in her dormitory to fellow students, talking through personal problems with them. She found this to be very fulfilling.

After finally receiving her degree in biology, Ann pondered what she wanted to do with her life. It was a serious dilemma. She had thought about medical school, with her biology degree, but decided a definite no to becoming a doctor. She thought about doing biological research, but she similarly decided no to that. She thought about teaching, but at this point that held little appeal.

Ann didn't know in what direction to go. She was deeply perplexed, realizing she had to decide something but having little clue of what to decide. She spent an entire weekend in her apartment praying, keeping herself cut off from everyone. She spent much of the weekend on her knees, asking God, "What am I supposed to do?" No telegram came from heaven, no definitive guidance.

But Ann reached one realization. She loved "meaningful conversations," talks with people about things that really mattered. She also loved the academic study of religion.

Ann decided, at length, to go to seminary. She picked Claremont, even though it was outside her denominational orbit. Ann resonated with seminary. It was apparent early that she was good at the things they did. The experience was greatly affirming.

Ann decided after a year, however, to move into her denominational loop, and she transferred to Princeton. She really liked it, especially her preaching class. Reading the Bible, interpreting what it says, fashioning that message for the present time, and developing exactly how to say it exhilarated Ann. She loved what she was doing.

There were at that time, however, few parish-minister women role models in her experience. As a seminary intern that summer, therefore, Ann worked with two women ministers in Trenton, New Jersey. She saw how they carried out ministry, and she realized she could do it, too. It was extremely affirming.

Graduating from seminary, Ann spent thirteen months looking for a pastoral job. She began to wonder, in her words, "if God had played a trick on me." In time, however, she took a part-time associate pastor's position in a midsize congregation in New Jersey, and a few years later an interim position in Maryland. Ann learned a lot about being a pastor in those positions, but neither was completely the right "match."

After several years, Ann moved to an internship in Maryland, where she and her effectiveness were essentially stifled. The combination did not work at all.

Then Ann saw an advertisement for an associate pastor position in what sounded like a wonderful church situation. She applied, along with many other applicants, and was offered the job. It turned out to be exactly the right match. In her words again, "Here, I don't have to hedge on the meaning of the gospel. Here, also, the congregation pushes me to do my best. And here I work with a group of people willing to take risks, not people who are in church primarily to play it safe." Ann loves it!

Charlie. Charlie was born a Jew, although one parent was not religious at all and the other cared little. Charlie prepared himself as a certified public accountant and subsequently started an accounting firm in New York City that, over a decade, became very successful.

Approaching middle age, Charlie decided to read the four Gospels in the Bible. He had never read much of the Bible before, certainly not the New Testament, and he was curious. He was immediately amazed. "The person I was reading about," he says, "could be none other than God incarnate."

It nevertheless took Charlie a year to feel that he believed in God, and two more years before he absorbed the Gospels enough to let "God incarnate" have a significant effect on his life. He started going to Brick Presbyterian Church in New York City, where he was baptized.

At church, Charlie asked for books to read. He read theology, church history, the whole Bible, meditations, and anything else he could find. He also became more active in the congregation.

At some not-entirely-definable point, Charlie became aware that God was calling him further into the church, possibly to go to seminary. When he was younger, he had been aware that accounting had been only his second or third choice as an optimum profession, but he had not been able to identify number one. Now he was beginning to know, even though it involved a slow, quiet debate with God.

One afternoon, the wife of a pastor at Brick Church came to Charlie's house to do some work with his wife. The pastor happened to come along. Charlie and the pastor sat together for two and a half hours discussing ministry. That afternoon was a decisive turning point for Charlie; he never stopped thinking about it afterward.

Charlie did not tire of his accounting work. In fact, he loved it. One of his accounts was the musical group, the Rolling Stones, and there were others just as interesting. He was in no hurry to leave accounting.

The most difficult matter for Charlie was to convince himself, "What we have is enough!" Could he and his wife and daughter sell the accounting firm, go to seminary, and be all right? He was struggling with what was a fundamental anxiety for him. At near middle age with a family, he found that that anxiety took on an entirely different perspective.

Charlie enrolled in seminary, however, and now, having passed Hebrew and a full year of study, is aimed at his second career, at what he believes is his first vocation.

Kate. In college, Kate majored in biology and music, a dual program that was not easy to piece together. She realized as she graduated, however, that she had no interest in spending her life in either field. She was much perplexed that she had devoted her undergraduate career to two areas that would lead her nowhere.

Kate agonized. She prayed. Up to this point, her religious faith had been mostly private. Though she had grown up in the church, she had not associated with a church in college.

A particular Sunday morning found Kate worshiping in a congregation attended by numerous musicians, a very traditional congregation that would not even have considered employing a female pastor. As she sat in worship, however, listening to the leaders lead, the idea suddenly came to her, "Is this what I ought to do?"

After worship, the idea persisted. Kate's biology training had made her realize that she knew how to teach. Her music talent would be useful in the church. Peer counseling work she had done in her college sorority had made her know that she had an aptitude for working with people in knitting their lives together.

Her decision suddenly came to her as a natural. All the pieces fit. Kate went to seminary with a vocational excitement that has never diminished, and she is now a pastor in a congregation.

Joel. Joel was an actor. He had grown up in a preacher's household. He had a wonderful speaking voice and strong talents in oral communication. He chose to get a B.A. in theater and an M.F.A. in acting.

Because his father was a U.C.C. minister, Joel implicitly realized through life that this was something he could do, and that he could do it and remain a "real person." But there was no urging. He cannot remember a conversation when his father mentioned it.

Joel married while in graduate school in Austin, Texas. One day, because of a vague inner urging, he took a long walk around the Austin Presbyterian Theological Seminary campus. He sat down and tried to figure out his interest in the place. Finally, he walked away, having done nothing in particular, but realizing that it had been a deliberate act.

Both Joel and his wife, an actress, accepted work in New York City. Joel took what he calls a "survival job," working for an investment firm, while his wife was employed in traveling theater.

One day, with a similar inner urge as he had felt in Austin, Joel transported himself to the Union Theological Seminary campus and walked around. He went to the information desk and procured a seminary catalogue. He got home that day and discussed with his wife what he had done. Nothing more happened, although his wife, much more than he, seemed to sense that something would.

After a year in New York, both husband and wife took jobs

with Stage One Children's Theatre in Louisville, Kentucky. This was their opportunity to be together, not for one to be traveling regularly, so they purchased a house. They decided they needed to find a church in Louisville and to get active. They visited several churches, joining one. They became involved quickly, mostly with the young adults.

They came into conversation one evening with a seminary student who took particular interest in their story. This student had been a coast guard helicopter pilot for a number of years and had come to seminary in midcareer. He strongly encouraged Joel to take the step. Joel wasn't sure, but he definitely started thinking about it. He visited Louisville Presbyterian Seminary. He talked with his pastor about it, still inquiring. "What's the harm in applying?" he thought to himself, still not sure that this was what he would do. He was accepted and was offered a presidential scholarship, indicating that the seminary thought very highly of his credentials.

Joel says that the call from God was very hard to pin down, very hard to articulate—that it was mostly a vague feeling. The thing that finally convinced him, however, was the community of people at his church. Young adults, youth, others—as soon as they heard what he was considering, they encouraged him. They seemed to know more clearly than he. He decided to do it.

Joel was asked to do an internship in his congregation during his first year of seminary, working with youth. This experience affirmed his decision even more. He worked at the Presbyterian Church (U.S.A.) headquarters in Louisville during his second year and as a prison intern in his third. Everything told him that his decision was right. Upon graduation, Joel procured a position as an associate pastor and was ordained.

Alice. Alice was born a Jehovah's Witness. She spent her early life "knocking on doors and manipulating people with my cute little smile." Before she was three, she had sold hundreds of Watchtower magazines.

Alice's parents separated. She and her sister lived with their mother.

When Alice was about nine, her mother went off to live with a man, leaving the two daughters with their grandparents. The grandparents provided a good home, but Alice got in with the wrong friends. Her life began to turn crazy. By junior high school, Alice had become "a bad girl."

Alice's mother returned home. Alice didn't like the person her mother had become. She deeply resented her having left. Alice's life continued its downward spiral.

In high school, there was a guidance counselor who took special interest in Alice. One day, the counselor said to her, "If you go on the way you are, you'll mess up your life." The guidance counselor handed Alice her professional card and said, "My phone number is on that card. Keep it. When you need me, call. I'll be waiting." Alice kept the card.

Soon after this, when Alice was about fifteen, she ran away from home. She took to the streets, living in abandoned houses, homes for runaways, and anywhere else she could find. She was, in her words, "exploring and having fun, and living out the pain I felt toward my mother."

Months later, Alice went home. She was greeted by her mother and a police officer. The officer arrested her and locked her up for about two hours. She stayed home a week and then was gone again. She didn't want to be out on the streets, but she felt she had no home.

After many days of despair, Alice literally knelt down at a street corner and prayed to God to send her someone who would love her. After finishing her prayer, she discovered a quarter in her pocket. She also found the business card the high school guidance counselor had given her months earlier. She called.

The counselor met Alice and drove her to the counselor's

upper-middle class home in a prosperous neighborhood. As they entered, the counselor said, "As long as you like, this is your home." No conditions, no requirements.

Alice settled into an entirely new life. The counselor had more money than Alice had ever been around before, and she apparently had little reservation in spending it on Alice. Alice bought clothes, shoes—anything she wanted. She still ran away at least once a month, but the counselor would find her. The counselor was not a religious person and attended no church.

Alice was popular in high school. She loved to sing and joined a gospel choir that sang in churches. She found herself really uncomfortable in church. The shouting, the praising God, the spiritual excitement was not for her.

When high school was over, Alice went to college. She joined a campus Bible study, thinking it was time to "do God a favor." She decided to affiliate with a church. She found she really liked it: "There was so much love everywhere I went, and there were people of every race and nationality, and that was what I wanted to be part of." She finally called the pastor late one night and told him she was ready to be baptized. The pastor was ecstatic! He told her to meet him at the church at 3:00 A.M. When she got there, the church was full of people! The pastor had called around and asked them to come. Alice was overwhelmed.

She was in for quick disillusionment, however. She had expected the world to be different after her baptism. She had expected a glow of light, a shining universe. Unfortunately, the world was the same. In fact, if anything, it was more difficult: she felt pressure now to stop partying and to turn away from her boyfriend. The church also wanted her to stop going home on weekends and instead do door knocking and solicitation for them. "That rubbed me the wrong way," she says, "so I soon left." She transferred to college in another city because the members of the church would not leave her alone.

In the new city, her boyfriend's mother asked her to start a youth group in her church. Alice consented. The church then asked her to teach youth Sunday school. She did, and she joined the choir. The pastor preached sermons that penetrated her heart, but he soon left to go elsewhere. Alice left too.

The new pastor called her for lunch and asked her if she would come back, but Alice said no. The church kept mailing her bulletins signed by children with notes on how much they missed her.

Alice finished college and graduated. She took a job with a television station as a production assistant.

The church pastor called her for lunch again. "I need you to help me," he said, very directly. Then he looked her straight in the eye with a piercing gaze and said, "I know you are called." Alice trembled, shaking. She completely lost her composure. As the conversation went forward, the pastor addressed her as "preacher." She got up and left.

On New Year's Eve, Alice was at home alone feeling upset and unhappy with her life. She began praying to God to help her. She prayed earnestly! She prayed hard. Finally, she said, "God, whatever you want me to do, I'm ready." She felt a rush of energy. She started running around the house, dancing, jumping, this way, that way.

She called the pastor she had met with before. She went to his house. As he stood in the door, he looked at her and started crying. They hugged each other for a long time. Her first words were, "How do I begin this process?"

She and the pastor started meeting once a week. Alice was accepted in a seminary. Three years later, Alice graduated, and has now worked in four different church settings.

What do you hear in these stories? I hear variety, variety in the people called. It can happen to anyone. God's call is not confined to likely candidates. I hear variety in the ways the call comes. Each instance is unique. Your call will be different from everyone else's. God does not have a standardized procedure.

I hear talent matching. Each of these people brought something significant to the vocation. They were not fully prepared, but they also were not fully bereft. Each had strength. Each began with something significant to give, whether it was a skill for teaching or an experimental knowledge of being down-and-out, coupled with a capacity to learn.

I hear also a small voice, quiet but persistent. A beckoning that will not go away. An irresistible urge. There are no words spoken through clouds, no convincing proofs, no signs. But there are compelling indicators.

Is there a compelling factor that God is calling you? That is the question you are facing right now. That is why you are reading this book.

In the four chapters that follow, I will describe what I have found to be *the essence* of being a pastor, the fundamental things we are called to do. Think about them. Think about spending your life doing them. Will they motivate you? Will they be more important to you than making money? Do you find them a critical part of human living? Will they carry you through the difficult times? Is God calling you to be a pastor?

Chapter 3

The Holy One in Our Midst

We Christians believe that God dwells "with us." God is not a distant, aloof Being, cut off from life, but One who resides close by, touching and shaping what happens, calling life forward toward God's purposes. God walks with us "through the valley of the shadow of death" (Ps. 23:4, RSV). If we ascend to heaven, God is there; if we make our beds in Sheol, God is there; if we take the wings of the morning and travel to the uttermost parts of the sea, even there God's hand leads us and God's right hand holds us (Psalm 139). God speaks to us through the words of prophets, preachers, and strangers. Jesus, Immanuel, is "God with us." In the figure of the Holy Spirit, the church professes God's continuing Presence in our life.

The feature that makes the church different from all other organizations in society is its profession of The Holy. We believe there is with us One we cannot see but whose Presence is the most important matter in life. The main thing we are looking for when we enter church is not the teaching, not the preaching, not the music, but an encounter with God. This, far beyond all else, will make members of a congregation know that their church life is for real. Without this, members will feel that their church life is simply one more social-recreational-educational activity among many.

The first role of the pastor is to identify, meaningfully and

27

powerfully, the presence of God in our lives. It is not a matter of "conjuring up" God, of manipulating God into an appearance, as some faith traditions try to do. It is identifying and celebrating the God who is already present among us.

Thousands of people in our time are hungry for "spiritual connection." Huge numbers attend search groups, in church or otherwise, seeking to make contact. Many have turned to meditation, to chanting, to dance, to ecstasy, to incense, to candles—indeed, to a whole body of "spiritual disciplines"—hoping to find the experience they need.

Unfortunately, much of the searching is in dead-end places for a god who is entirely too small. We look to establish special connection with a god who will help us get what we want, help us through the demands and stresses of the week, help us win our competitions and rivalries with other people, help us lose twenty pounds, help us pass a test or hit a free throw. Most of the games we want God to play are quite self-centered and trivial.

Society has lately been obsessed with angels. Angel books fill the religion shelves of local bookstores. Angel symbols find their way onto jewelry, clothing, and bedposts. But the angels we want are angels that shower blessing, not angels that speak challenge, as biblical angels did. Biblical angels were awesome, fear-invoking, leaving those to whom they spoke thoroughly claimed and commissioned to tasks they often did not want! What we look for in our time is a connection with God that will guarantee us safety and success and pleasure, not one that will call us into demanding service.

The primary job of the pastor is to unveil God's presence in human life. The importance of this cannot be overstated. It is easily the most significant task the pastor is called to carry out.

Of course, people find it easy to see God in a beautiful sunset, in the design of a magnificent flower, in a waterfall, in a lovely work of music, in a newborn baby. It doesn't take a pastor to point out God's presence in these places.

However, other appearances are more subtle—for instance, in *human reclamation.* Not long ago, I watched six women graduate from the education/rehabilitation program of a prison halfway house. These women had formerly lived lives, as one woman said, "out in that wild jungle," on the streets amid drugs, alcohol, and crime. On graduation day, they were literally straining forward to find new life. Of course, they were anxious; they were frightened. They clung to one another for support, but they knew that God is in the reclamation business, that they could become new people. So they marched ahead, trusting that they would find strength. They wanted more than anything else to become people they themselves could be proud of.

The graduation ceremony happened in my church's sanctuary on a Saturday afternoon. It was both humble and elegant. The next morning, I told my congregation, "I cannot be sure whether we will find God here today, but I am absolutely certain that I found God here yesterday." There were six lives trusting St. Paul's promise that the trumpet shall sound and the dead shall be raised; six hearts believing that resurrection to new life could be theirs. God was most definitely there.

God is also present in *human endurance.* I knew a woman whose husband and only child died in the same year— he of a heart attack, she in an auto accident. The woman grieved mightily, despairing for her dearly beloved. Her life became an empty shell, dreadfully lonely. She missed them every moment. But, after a time, she arose to her feet and got herself moving again. She found new relationship and new purpose. She never forgot her great loss, but she discovered her new gain. She had become a healthy, thriving woman again by the time I knew her, rich in relationship and living a clear purpose. I asked her how she had done it, how she had managed to rise from the depths. Her reply was quite simple, "God was with me. I called on the Lord, and God became my strength." I have no doubt that she was right. I have seen that story played out many times.

God is present in *human sharing.* I once watched a very poor family of five take into their home an equally poor family of four after the latter family's house burned. It was a tight existence. There wasn't enough food or space, but generosity ruled and turned what little the hosts had into more than enough for everyone. Their "we-can-make-it-work!" spirit was greater than any lack. Jesus fed the multitude on five loaves and two fish; God was surely there.

God is also present in *forgiveness.* Nearly every war fought between nations provides stories of soldiers who related to one another, supported one another, helped one another across the battle lines. Enemies became friends; opponents reconciled. Although these stories are anathema to those in charge of the battle, they are God's miracles to those who took part.

The biblical prophets even found God's presence in *judgment.* Isaiah, for instance, warned that a multitude of nations were going to march against Jerusalem to destroy it, and that God would be in the midst of the multitude.

> The multitude of your foes shall be like small dust,
>   and the multitude of [oppressors] like flying chaff.
> In an instant, suddenly,
>   you will be visited by the LORD of hosts
> with thunder and earthquake and great noise,
>   with whirlwind and tempest, and the flame
>   of a devouring fire.
>
> (Isa. 29:5–6)

I would not recommend this as standard fare in your congregation—that is, don't be tempted to copy Isaiah!—but the point to realize is that God's presence is often found well beyond our expectations.

Hebrews 13:2 says, "Do not neglect to show hospitality to strangers, for by doing that some have entertained angels without knowing it." God's presence is sometimes found in the sojourner, the foreigner, the one who views life through eyes different from ours—the immigrant, the refugee, the Jew, the Muslim.

God's presence is found as believers read and deliberate the Bible. Through the Bible's words we hear God's Word. We hear it through study, through preaching, through worship, through prayer; through the Word spoken, the Word sung, the Word enacted, the Word danced. The Bible speaks with a clarity, an incisiveness, a beckoning that is unique. Christians place the Bible front and center in worship because it is through this book, we believe, that God most dependably and repeatedly speaks. If you go to seminary, you will spend a huge part of your time studying the Bible. The church recognized long, long ago that it is primarily through this book that God dwells with the church, full of grace and truth, speaking call and challenge.

Your first role as a pastor will be to unveil the presence of God, to develop special eyes for seeing, special language for telling. You will invite the faithful to find in their everyday a larger dimension, and you will bid them to interpret what happens in the language and mindset of The Holy.

It is important to avoid a too-easy glibness; there is more than enough of that around already, and the church doesn't need anymore from you. You will need to avoid descending into a self-righteousness that comes from your claim to know more about God than any of us knows. You will need to be sure that the Other you are identifying is God and not god, One high and lifted up and not one trivialized.

You will need to search every event that happens in your life, looking for what most people do not see. You will need to measure everything against the biblical paradigms of God's activity. You will need to nurture a sixth sense that you were born with but probably lost somewhere along the way, a sense of awe and wonder at the mundane. Seminary won't teach this sensitivity to you. The professors will encourage it, but they do not know how to teach it. You will have to find it in yourself.

If this search is meaningful for you, if it touches your imagination and challenges your spirit, if it will pour cause into your own life and give you vitality, then consider strongly whether God is calling you to be a pastor.

Chapter 4

The Miracle of Resurrection

*G*od raises people from the dead. Because of that reality, the Bible was written. On that faith, the church lives.

God raises people from the dead. In Egypt there was a band of slaves, descendants of migratory relatives who came from the land of Canaan. Measured against the greatness of Egypt, these slaves were a tiny crew, powerless, insignificant, zero in importance—unnoticed by the world. But God noticed. God heard their cries from slavery, the laments of their labor. God listened. And God raised them from the dead, delivering them at the Red Sea, leading them through a great and terrible wilderness with its scorpions and fiery serpents, and making them a powerful nation, mighty and populous, as numerous as the stars in the sky or the grains of sand on the seashore.

God raises people from the dead. For more than forty years, Israel had been in exile in Babylon—a captive people in a strange land, taken there after Nebuchadnezzar's destruction of Jerusalem. They had hung their musical instruments upon the trees, unable to sing the Lord's song in this godforsaken place. But Persia, in time, overthrew Babylon, one great power toppling another. And God sent a prophet who declared to Israel, "Make straight in the desert a highway for your God! Prepare the way! I am taking you home! Returning you to where you belong! To reconstitute your cities. To rebuild your walls. To refashion your community. To return your life." By a much celebrated trek, Israel went home—the people of God taking up residence a second time in the promised land.

God raises people from the dead. "Two men in dazzling clothes suddenly stood beside us," the women reported. "We were terrified and bowed our faces to the ground. But they said to us, 'Why do you look for the living among the dead? He is not here. He has risen'" (from Luke 24:4–5). "When he was at the table with them, he took bread, blessed and broke it, and gave it to them. Then their eyes were opened, and they recognized him; and he vanished from their sight" (Luke 24:30–31).

God raises people from the dead. "As in Adam all die, so also in Christ shall all be made alive" (1 Cor. 15:22, RSV). "The trumpet will sound, and the dead will be raised imperishable, and we will be changed" (1 Cor. 15:52, RSV).

God raises people from the dead. Mary Magdalene, Joanna, Mary the mother of James, and the other women with them went running, terrified, back from the tomb. Finding the apostles, the women told them what had happened—about the two men in dazzling clothes, the words spoken, the empty tomb. So excited were they that the words poured from their lips! But the apostles, after listening, discounted the entire matter, thinking it an idle tale of overly excitable females. Only one apostle, Peter, got up and went to the tomb to see. It was after that that the church realized that it almost missed the most important news in the history of the world, and that perhaps it needed to take women more seriously.

God raises people from the dead. Saul was a devoted apostle of God, a Pharisee. He was certain that this new sect of Jesus-followers was an enemy to God, a lawless band of renegades whose purpose was to dilute and destroy true faith. Saul devoted all of his youthful vigor to persecuting them mercilessly, uncovering Christians in this place and that and binding them for jail. Saul pursued this life wholeheartedly until, on the Damascus Road, Christ appeared to him, asking, "Saul, Saul, why do you persecute me?" It was then that Saul became Paul, a man with new eyes, a new mind, a new heart. Saul transformed from being the great persecutor of Christians to being the leading missionary for Christ.

God raises people from the dead. On Tuesday and Friday evenings, about a hundred men and women gather at my church. They tell their stories to one another, who they have been and who they want to become. They talk about what the past few days have been like, their temptations, their struggles. They voice support for one another, affirm one another. They pray. They know they are in a life-or-death struggle. They know what failure will bring. They know the destructive power of the demons against which they contend. They come in search of a new way of life, a way that will sustain them instead of destroy them. Some have been sober ten years, fifteen years, twenty years. They hold good jobs and enjoy happy families; their lives are far different from what they used to be. Yes, it can happen! They act as mentors for the newer ones, special friends in the struggle. They are there to testify: yes, you can become a new person. It's a long, hard fight, requiring every shred of strength one can muster, a fight that is never over, but it can be won. If death is not stronger than the power of God, certainly alcohol addiction is not either.

God raises people from the dead. The Kentucky Refugee Ministry was born in my church. In recent years, the Refugee Ministry has resettled more than five hundred international refugees per year in the northern Kentucky region. At first they came from Vietnam, Romania, and Somalia; then from Bosnia, Kosovo, and Albania. Now they come from Cuba, Haiti, and Sudan. Resettling in a strange culture with a strange language is very, very hard. Refugees have to work, to be determined, to drive themselves, but the stories that emerge are incredible. One refugee is now a civil engineer who digs very big holes in the ground for hotels and parking garages. Another is a restaurant owner widely known for the elegance of his fare. Another is a surgeon. Another is the manager of an auto repair shop. Another is the owner of a multimillion dollar computer business. The list is long. They all came to this country out of violence and persecution, looking for a new future, not knowing if that was possible, but hoping. They are now living monuments to what can happen.

God raises people from the dead. In my office door walks a couple whose marriage is in trouble. They don't have the same fervor for each other they used to have. They both lead very busy lives, and by the time they get together at the end of the day, they are tired and worn out. They don't know what to talk about. There are a few things they enjoy together, but mostly he goes his way and she goes hers. He says that she criticizes him too much, constantly finding things wrong. She says that he is overbearing, wanting to boss the whole family. They don't want to split. Neither has any wish to live alone, and both cringe at the idea of getting back into the spouse hunt. But they have lost each other and can't find their way back. Can I help? Is it possible to discover a new relationship—the intimacy, commitment, and mystery of which rich marriage is made? Is the struggle worth the try, or should they just end it right now? How many times has that scene played its way through my pastoral life!

God raises people from the dead. Two years ago, I taught a class of laypeople on the subject "Images of Resurrection across the Bible." We looked at Genesis 1, at God's creation of good, good, good, good, good, good and very good, with the strongly implied promise that this was not just where our life began but also where it is headed. We looked at Psalm 90, at the psalmist's belief that our "threescore years and ten" are imbedded in the "from everlasting to everlasting" of God. We looked at the parable of the last judgment in Matthew 25. We looked at the narrative of the empty tomb in Mark 16. We looked at Paul's exciting story of the resurrection in 1 Corinthians 15. We looked at the new heaven and new earth of Revelation 21—all contributing to the Bible's conviction that what we experience on this earth is not the final chapter. When the last class was over, the students erupted in spontaneous applause. It was not polite applause but joyous applause, cheering applause. They were cheering not for the teacher nor for the way the class had been taught. They were cheering God, God's gift of a future, for the conviction held by Christians across two thousand years that what comes next is not an empty nothing. It will be the Creator's second creation, promised to be even more rich, more splendid, than the first.

God raises people from the dead. Karl Barth was right, that the dominant question people are asking as they enter the doors of the church sanctuary on Sunday morning is, "Is it really true?" Can I find new life? Is there some meaning that can redeem the hectic struggle of my daily world? Is there a worthwhile purpose behind the disputes? Can I become less angry, less upset, less volatile? Can I forgive more easily? Can I love more fully, have fun more joyfully? Can I relate to people more meaningfully? Can I give myself away and thereby find myself? These are the questions people bring to church.

Your role as a pastor is to expect resurrection—not because of human power but because of God's power. To believe that people and communities can change and become new. To know that minds can shift and that lives can turn corners. To assert that churches and other communities can become what they have never been before. To invest yourself in challenging people to the unlikely.

When you look into the eyes of another human being, you will need to be able to see possibilities not previously realized. What might this person become? To what heights might she or he rise? The easy path is to expect what is; the pastor's path is to expect what might be.

You will need to be something of a naive fool, one of those strange creatures who sees possibilities where no one else sees anything. Some of the people who come to Alcoholics Anonymous meetings look pretty hopeless. Some have wasted, bedraggled bodies shriveled with mistreatment; minds that struggle to focus and make sense. But they come because they hope. They hope for a new future, a different way, believing in God's power to provide it. You will need to be a person who hopes with them, believing with every ounce of conviction in your heart that God raises people from the dead.

In the book of the prophet Ezekiel, chapter 37, Ezekiel says that the hand of the Lord took hold of him. God lifted him up and set him down in the middle of a valley, a valley full of bones. The spirit of the Lord led Ezekiel around over the valley, and he saw that there were many bones lying in the valley, and that they were very dry.

Every ancient Israelite reader would have known that the valley referred to was the Valley of Jezreel—the large, fertile expanse in northern Israel west of the Sea of Galilee. Not only was this valley a favorite growing land of farmers; it was also a favorite battleground for armies. Most of Israel is hill country, and it is hard for a marching army to fight on a hillside. But the Valley of Jezreel provides a perfect location for conquest. Wars have been fought there throughout the generations, and, in fact, the ultimate battle of all history, the battle of Armageddon, between the angels of God and earth's forces of evil, is projected to be fought there at the end of time. Ezekiel's valley would have been, in the ancient reader's mind, the Valley of Jezreel, and dry bones scattered across the valley would have been the result of a monumental conflict.

God looked at the bones and said to Ezekiel, "Mortal, can these bones live?"

Ezekiel, looking at the bones, could see no way! How

could totally dry bones come to life? How could anything this dead have a living future? Thinking it could never happen, but not wanting to speak disparagingly of God's power, Ezekiel replied, "O Lord GOD, you know" (v. 3).

God said to Ezekiel: "'Prophesy to these bones, and say to them, O dry bones, hear the word of the LORD'" (v. 4). This was not the word of any human assessment but the word of God's intention. "'Thus says the Lord GOD to these bones: I will cause breath to enter you, and you shall live. I will lay sinews on you, and will cause flesh to come upon you, and cover you with skin, and put breath in you, and you shall live'" (vv. 5–6).

Ezekiel spoke as he had been told. To his utter amazement, suddenly there was a noise, a rattling. The bones came together, bone to its bone. There were sinews on them, and flesh came upon them and skin covered them. Then God breathed the breath of life into the bones, and the bones lived! They stood upon their feet, an exceeding great army!

Through Ezekiel we clearly see the pastor's task: To prophesy! To preach! To invoke! To call forth God's resurrecting power! To pray! To beckon! Doubting all the while that it will really happen, to issue forth great faith! Inwardly disbelieving, to summon God's resurrecting work. As clearly as any text in the Bible, this story of Ezekiel sets forth the pastor's charge.

It is strange business. People will think you are weird and naive, an impossible optimist. The task will confound good sense, sound planning. You will spend a lot of time on dead-end causes, on people for whom there is no hope, on dreams that can't possibly work. The world will wonder seriously about your sanity.

But if you have inside you the capability for this kind of unrealism, the capacity to believe when there is no visible reason to believe, then consider whether God is calling you to be a pastor.

Chapter 5

Direction

*T*he task of every Christian pastor is to call people, in God's name, to be disciples of Jesus Christ, to speak Christ's bidding, "Follow me."

To some, that will mean urging people to follow Christ's rules, to obey Jesus' teachings, to do exactly what he said. The more rigorously we obey, the better disciples we are. Discipleship is compliance with Christ's words.

I do not understand discipleship that way. Discipleship, to me, means letting Christ set the direction—taking my fundamental cues from his leading. Discipleship is a pilgrimage down a path that Jesus picks.

"Direction" is something a great many people have trouble with. Albert Einstein once said, *"Perfection of means and confusion of ends* seems to characterize our age" (John W. Gardner, *On Leadership* [New York: The Free Press, a division of Macmillan, 1990], p. 11, italics mine). In other words, we in modern times have become masters at *how to get there,* but we have a much harder struggle discerning where *there* needs to be. We are experts at negotiating the journey, but we don't know the destination.

A chief domain of the pastor is *direction.*

I have talked with hundreds of church members about their lives. Direction is the most frequent confusion. "Idolatry" in

41

our time means, more than anything else, setting for one's life the wrong direction, looking for fulfillment from gods whose promises are empty, heading somewhere that turns out to be nowhere. We human beings are really good at it.

The most common wrong direction is *passion for money,* the belief that wealth will make us content, happy, and secure on this earth.

Poverty is awful. It should never be glamorized. The Bible never treats it as a good thing, and neither should we.

Enough money is a great blessing. God gave Israel "the land flowing with milk and honey" and told them to enjoy it, to make themselves thoroughly at home in it, to exhilarate in it. Possessing money is not evil. People who have money and who use it well do us all an enormous favor.

But *enough,* especially regarding money, is probably the most elusive concept in our culture. Most of us are not very good at knowing what it means.

More than a few lives in a church congregation will be directed primarily, and in some cases almost totally, toward making money. This will be the most important pursuit, and all else will be secondary. Egos will be formed; self-evaluations will be based on how much money one can make. It is a faulty direction. Money makes promises it cannot fulfill. It can create power, status, and glamour, but it cannot create contentment, happiness, or security. It takes most of us a few years in life, and perhaps some financial success, to figure that out.

I had a young businessman come into my office recently to tell a story. "A few nights ago," he said, "I spent one of my rare evenings at home. I lay down on my two-year-old's bed to read *Goodnight Moon* before he went to sleep. He especially liked the part about the little old lady who was whispering, 'hush'; he would put his finger to his mouth and quietly say, 'Shhh. . . .' I must have read that page twenty times. In the middle of the book, the thought hit me, 'Why don't I do this more often? What am I missing?'

"And a few minutes later, when my son was asleep, I flopped in a comfortable chair in the living room and had an hour's conversation with my wife over what is going on in her life—not my life, *her* life: the books she is reading, the course she is taking, the friends she has made, the challenges and joys of spending most of the day with our children. And I found myself thinking again, 'Why don't I do this more often?'"

His question, of course, was a question of direction.

The *compulsion to win* is another wrong direction. Competitiveness can be a highly addictive drug.

Our culture worships winning. The winner will be glorified and exalted, make all the headlines, take all the prizes. Less-than-winners disappear into nonexistence. I search in vain through the sports pages of my local newspaper for a single article on the challenges of maintaining one's spirit and motivation through losing. Losers are disdained, devalued, shunned, told what they should have done to win!

There will be people in a congregation who work sixty, seventy, seventy-five hours a week trying to make sure they are winners. Even worse, there will be some who will do anything necessary to win, including deception, exploitation, lawbreaking, and evil. What sort of victory is that?

My wife and I once lived in a community that sought beyond all else to produce highly successful people, world-class achievers who would reflect well on the town. Young people of industry and promise were lauded, given awards, and featured in the public spotlight. Lesser achievers were ignored, told by implication that they weren't worth attention. Many of those lesser achievers struggled to find meaning in their existence. What was it worth to be in the middle of the pack? That community was not a good place for the average Joe or Susie to grow up.

Christ sets our direction. He called it love—love that

happens in human relationship; love that expresses itself in self-giving.

There is nothing on this earth more important to us than other people. They have the power to make the sky blue, the stars bright, the garden beautiful. They offer profound meaning and fulfillment. They make time worthwhile and hours rich. Meaningful companionship was God's greatest gift in the creation.

Jesus calls us to relate to other people in self-giving. "The Son of Man came not to be served but to serve, and to give his life a ransom for many" (Mark 10:45). To follow a self-giving Christ in a self-serving world is Jesus' direction. To live lives that enrich other lives. To care about what happens to other people. To hear them when they speak, to pay attention when they communicate. To know when they are crying, to feel pain when they hurt. To laugh with them, rejoice with them.

The most pathetic thing I see in life is people who live their lives alone, people who essentially have no one. They can be outcasts who wander the streets. They can be children to whom no one pays any special attention. They can be elderly people in nursing homes. They can be a wife or husband drowned in satisfying their spouse's success agenda.

Jesus calls us to know one another intimately and well: to walk with one another, to see one another, to hear one another, to give ourselves for one another, to love one another.

A fundamental task of the pastor is to point direction: through sermons, through teaching, through conversations, through stories, through questions. Some people will turn away sorrowful, unable to change their route. Others will find new life.

If inviting people to travel a road you believe in, a direction they have not thought about before in quite the way you present it, is something you would find valuable to do with your life, then ask yourself seriously if God is calling you to be a pastor.

Chapter 6

Sacred Privilege

*I*n Louisville, Kentucky, there are five hundred front doors where I am welcome to knock. The people who answer will be genuinely glad to see me. They will invite me inside and ask me to sit down. Talking with them, I can ask almost any question I wish—not quite anything, but almost. I can ask about family, about health, about job, about relationships, about meaning, about future—almost anything. In most cases, I will get a sincere answer. The people will open the interior of their lives to me, letting me know what is inside. They will discuss deeply personal matters.

When we finish, they will be profoundly appreciative that I came. They will be grateful that I asked the questions. They will thank me for having spent our time together this way. As I leave, they will invite me back again to do the same thing all over.

If a policeman sat in their living room and asked those questions, the people would be scared to death. If a lawyer did it, they would be highly suspicious. If a doctor did it, they would think something was wrong with their health. But when the pastor does it, the questions are entirely welcome. The pastor has an entrée into people's lives that no one else in society has. The pastor can explore the recesses, walk the sacred territory. Such permission is given to few others, but is almost automatically given to the pastor.

I am convinced that the most pervasive psychopathology in American society is *loneliness,* people who are not known by anyone. I meet them all the time, people who have fascinating, moving stories of which no one inquires.

I've known a man in my congregation who grew up in probably the most violent, exploitive, dishonest family situation I have ever heard of. This man learned daily lessons in parental anger, in total uncaring, in poverty, in violence. And yet, by the force of his own determination, he is different. He vowed as an early adolescent that he was never going to be like his father, and he has fulfilled his promise! He struggles with the demons, directing himself consciously to be the person he wants to be, but he pulls it off. I consider it a privilege to have been admitted into his story. And I was shocked to learn that I was just about the first person who had ever wanted to know.

There is a woman who is the daughter of a very poor Japanese family who made their way to this country. They were "rounded up," with other Japanese, at the beginning of World War II and kept in a detention camp. This was her childhood. She is a gold mine of memory, a rich vision into our nation's past. But, in her words, "No one asks, so I rarely tell."

Our society talks much better than it listens. Telling about ourselves is something a lot of us do well; formulating good questions for other people and listening carefully to their answers is something most of us do poorly. The person who will ask the right questions and then listen is a sacred commodity.

I don't in any way look forward to deaths and funerals, but I have come to anticipate one thing that can happen at the time of a death and funeral. Dad passes away at a ripe old age, and Mom, a couple of sons and daughters with spouses, four or five grandchildren, a brother, a sister, and maybe a cousin gather for the funeral. I assemble them in a room where we all agree to spend a couple of hours. I ask them to talk about Dad. To tell a story they remember. To tell about an instance that particularly characterizes him. To tell about their relationship with him.

The outcome is virtually always magic. The family relives its interior. Joys, hurts, laughter, tears—they feed on one another. Stories are told that bind the family together—rich stories some have not heard before. Everyone thanks me profoundly when we are finished. All I did was initiate it. I feel I have had a privileged seat in a sacred place.

This opening we have into people's lives is an enormous privilege to be nurtured with great respect and care, never to be abused.

I worked in the same town with the pastor of a large congregation who had an urgent need to tell to anyone who would listen the private information he had learned from his church members. One day, I sat at a lunch table and heard him describe to seven or eight of us a totally private conversation he had had with a man in his congregation I had known since childhood. I was appalled! He should never have told anything, much less everything! His stated rationale at the end was, "I wanted you to know this so you too could pray for him." In fact, this pastor needed to feel important, and to be able to tell the latest confidential information on his parishioner made him feel that way. What a gross misuse of our sacred privilege!

The pastor has an entrée into people's lives that almost no one else has. You can explore the interior, hear the stories. You can ask nearly any question you want. You can get to know people in a full and wonderful sense. If you value this privilege and if you will honor it, knowing what not to repeat later, I suggest you consider whether God is calling you to be a pastor.

Chapter 7

Words, Words

*I*n Genesis 1, God creates the universe. God takes a dark blob of watery chaos and fashions the entire creation. God creates light. God creates air. God creates sun and moon and stars. God creates dry land. God creates vegetation, trees, and plants. God creates birds and fish. God creates animals and living creatures. And at the end God creates man and woman, human beings.

The power by which God brings all these things into being is very simple: God speaks. God utters a word. God declares, "Let there be . . . ," and, behold, there is . . . .

Words, according to this story, are magnificently powerful! They are the strongest force in the universe, the phenomenon with which all creativity begins. There is nothing more important than words, the things that get said. A carefully chosen word can create an entire world.

Our older son, Andy, has had tongue in cheek all his life. He loves to pull the right practical joke at the right moment. There was a time when Andy's high school class traveled to Florida for an underwater study. They went shallow-water diving in the ocean in search of data on something I don't remember. They traveled to and from Florida by bus.

On the return trip, the bus stopped at a fast-food restaurant in southern Georgia. The restaurant happened to be next to the local high school, and the bus arrived just as school was letting out for the day. As the busload was ordering, a group of girls from the high school arrived. Andy and several other boys struck up conversation. They told the girls they were the football team and cheerleaders from a high school in Kentucky, that they had just played two schools in Florida and beaten the stuffings out of both of them. The story got bigger the more they told it and the more the girls believed it. They had played against two of the largest high schools in Miami. They had scored seven touchdowns against one and nine against the other. Their defense never gave an inch. They were ready to be crowned state football champions of Florida.

In Andy's class was one particularly small boy who wore big horn-rimmed glasses. The kid was a bookworm, smart as he could be but in no way athletic. As the story began to wane, Andy spirited this kid forward out of the pack and introduced him to the girls as their all-state middle linebacker, the main force behind the team's defense, the guy who had singlehand-edly annihilated Florida quarterbacks on at least eleven occasions. Everyone was slapping this little kid on the back and proclaiming what a great football player he was, how central he was to the team's success.

When the busload finally left the fast-food restaurant, the tale was still intact. They had pulled it off, and they were delighted. Who knows what stories were told in that Georgia high school the next day!

But the most remarkable result was yet to come. The little "bookworm" with the horn-rimmed glasses took on an entirely new self-image. He now "belonged" as he never had before. He joked and laughed with his classmates as they continued to share the make-believe. He now became the hero of the bus, of the trip: "our champion middle linebacker." He enjoyed that status all the way back to Kentucky and beyond. The words, the mental ideas, had created a new reality.

Despite the attention given in recent years to "positive reinforcement" in the field of education, most people in our time still do not realize the powerfully creative force that resides right on the tips of our tongues. Frequently, my congregation's music director asks young church members to offer in worship music they have been learning to play or sing in their music lessons. We try to take care not to ask anyone who is likely to be embarrassed, but we also seek to signify that a church congregation is made up of a great variety of people, old and young, advanced and novice, accomplished and struggling, and that everyone, at least potentially, has a place in worship leadership.

When a twelve-year-old has played a piece on a violin or when a fourteen-year-old has sung, I nearly admonish the congregation: "If you appreciated what you just heard, don't simply turn to the person next to you and mutter, 'That was nice.' Get yourself up out of your pew when the service is over, march down to the front of the sanctuary, and tell that twelve-year-old or that fourteen-year-old how much you appreciated his or her music and how much you thank him or her for the work invested. That music did not drop out of the sky! The young person has been working on it for a long time, putting in the best possible effort. Acknowledge! Thank! Encourage! You will be amazed at how creative your few words of appreciation can be!" Some extremely talented young adults still come back and play or sing for us, remembering the encouragement they received much earlier in life.

I have been preaching for thirty-seven years, but I still feel a burst of motivation when someone says, "That sermon really spoke to me."

If you become a pastor, it will be absolutely essential for you to believe one hundred percent in the creative power of words. Words will be your primary tool, the dominant thing with which you will work. Words will create your success or your failure. If you believe that speech adds up to little more than just a bunch of empty words, then you probably should not set out to become a pastor.

As a pastor, you will experience someday a rather substantial identity crisis. You will walk into a hospital room. The person sick in the bed will be one of your church members. You will want sincerely to do something to help the person, something to make a difference.

As you stand there observing events in the room, you will wonder why you became a pastor. If you had become a doctor, you could help by analyzing the illness and prescribing what to do next. If you had become a nurse, you could help by adjusting the monitors and making sure the patient is comfortable. If you had become a dietitian, you could help by finding out what the patient wants for the next day's meals. If you had become a cleaning person, you could help by keeping dust off the floor. If you had become a pharmacist, you could help by making sure the correct prescriptions are delivered. If you had become an electrician, you could help by repairing the patient's table lamp. Everyone who passes through that room during your visit has a way to help, a designated function to serve—except you.

What are you there to do? It would be stupid for you to start sweeping the floor. Absurd for you to try to fix the lamp. Laughable for you to take the food order. Wrong for you to adjust the monitors. Downright dangerous for you to try to diagnose the illness. You have come to help. But what help can you provide? Everyone else's function is clear; what is yours?

I once teased a couple of Roman Catholic priest friends that their sacrament of extreme unction must have been devised by some priest who grew ultimately weary of arriving at deathbed scenes and finding nothing he could do. My friends smiled with at least a small touch of acknowledgment.

More than one pastor has left the ministry over this identity crisis. Ours is a utilitarian society. We value people by what they are able to do. What about the person who can't do anything; of what value is she or he? In many situations, that is the pastor.

The only way to survive as a pastor is to know in your heart, to be fully convinced, that words are the most important, the most creative, the most powerful phenomenon in the universe. With words you can say to that hospital patient that he or she is not alone in this illness, not traveling a solitary path, but that others walk there too. This happens to be the most important question in human life—is someone else there with me? With words you can face the full gravity of the situation and still convey the hope in your heart, in your faith. With words you can transcend the moment and invite the person into the larger realm of life's meaning. With words you can say that you care deeply, enough to take the time and energy to comprehend the person's experience.

There is nothing anyone will do that is more important. Words are the key to self-understanding, to relationship, to hope, to healing. If you don't say them, there may be no one else who does. Some of the most lonely people in the world lie in hospital beds surrounded by activity and attention. They are lonely because everything is being done for them except someone's paying attention, someone's speaking the right words. Many people, including doctors, do not consider themselves very good with words. Many people draw away from a sick or dying person instead of drawing closer. You, with words, can have enormous impact.

People come to me for pastoral counseling. Most of them are not afflicted by a serious psychological disease. A few are, and I try to refer those few to qualified counselors. Most come wanting me to help them "rearrange their words," to assist them in finding different mental images by which to analyze whatever situations they are facing, in drawing new word-pictures by which they can think about and approach a situation freshly. We often cannot change the actual situation—a person has lost his or her job, or is going through a divorce, or has a particularly rebellious child—but there is a lot we can change in the way we think about it. And that may be the most helpful contribution anyone can make.

Words create worlds. My entire thought-world, the world inside my brain, is made of language images: my understandings, my interpretations, my feelings, my middle-of-the-night-dreams, my middle-of-the-day insights, my decisions on what to do. I fear because I have in me the language of fear. I hope because my mind can articulate hope. I am confident because word images that evoke confidence reside within me. Language creates the universe in which I operate, and sometimes the greatest favor another person can do for me is give me a new language in which to think.

The pastor's chief domain is carefully chosen language. There will be substantial things you will be able to do for people—pick up medicine from the drug store, take a casserole to a family's home, help build a Habitat house, raise money for a community center—but by far your primary gifts will be through what you say. If you become a pastor, you will need to believe powerfully in the creative strength of words.

In Exodus 32–34, Moses travels back and forth between the bottom of Mount Sinai and the top. Up and down, up and down he goes. On the bottom, Moses speaks with the people about God: "You have sinned a great sin. But now I will go up to the LORD; perhaps I can make atonement for your sin" (Exod. 32:30). On the top, Moses speaks with God about the people: "Consider that this nation is your people! [You have said,] 'My presence will go with you, and I will give you rest'" (Exod. 33:13–14). On the bottom, Moses speaks again with the people, "You shall not make cast idols. You shall keep the festival of unleavened bread" (Exod. 34:17–18). On the top, Moses speaks again with God, "O Lord, I pray, let the Lord go with us. Although this is a stiff-necked people, pardon our iniquity and our sin, and take us for your inheritance" (Exod. 34:9).

As a pastor, you will do exactly what Moses did. You will talk with God about your people, and you will talk with your people about God, believing in both cases that your words have the power to create new worlds.

Talking with God about your people is called prayer. You will pray fervently for them, asking God to heal them, to teach them, to direct them, to accompany them, to still their animosities toward one another, to forgive them. You will organize and lead prayer groups. You will pray in worship. You will pray privately. And as you do so, you will need to keep in mind the little story Jesus told in Luke 18.

> [Jesus] said, "In a certain city there was a judge who neither feared God nor had respect for people. In that city there was a widow who kept coming to him and saying, 'Grant me justice against my opponent.' For a while he refused; but later he said to himself, 'Though I have no fear of God and no respect for anyone, yet because this widow keeps bothering me, I will grant her justice, so that she may not wear me out by continually coming.'" And [Jesus] said "Listen to what the unjust judge says. And will not God grant justice to his chosen ones who cry to him day and night?" (Luke 18:2–7)

Your prayers to God will need to be as persistent as that widow's begging. You will need to implore God over and over. You will need to show up day and night. You will need to become obnoxious, annoying—all because you believe profoundly that the great God of the universe values our words and responds to what we say.

In his book *On the Road* (New York: G. P. Putnam's Sons, 1985, pp. 1272–78), Charles Kuralt tells of the small chapel of Maria Angelorum in La Crosse, Wisconsin. At every moment of the day and night, Kuralt says, two nuns kneel before the altar in prayer. When the clock chimes the hour, the two sisters end their prayer by saying, "Bring peace to the world." They leave the chapel, and their place is taken by two other sisters. The chain of prayer is unbroken.

They are Franciscan Sisters of Perpetual Adoration. They have been praying without interruption for more than a hundred years! This began in 1878. Every hour of every day and night for more than a century, two sisters have been on their knees, side by side, always praying for the same thing—for an end to sickness and hunger, for an end to social injustice, for wisdom in high places, for their city and their country, for their friends, for their enemies, for all people, including you and me—always ending, "Bring peace to the world."

Sister Mileta, a scholar and writer, historian of the St. Rose convent, first took her place in this chain of prayer in 1915—hundreds of thousands of hours ago.

> **Kuralt:** Aren't you highly discouraged sometimes to think, for example, that you've been praying for world peace for a hundred years and there's been so little peace?
>
> **Sister Mileta:** Right. And we think the Lord must be discouraged, too, after all these years of wanting His kingdom to come and fill so many who are so far away. Yet discouragement, perhaps, should be a reason for still more fervent prayer, rather than for giving up.
>
> **Kuralt:** So you're just going to go on praying for another hundred years?
>
> **Sister Mileta:** Hopefully, yes. Hopefully, we can go on for another hundred years, and perhaps another hundred years, till the end of time.

If you become a pastor, you will need to be afflicted with the same persistence those nuns are, believing that your words have strong, creative effect in the heart of God.

Talking with your people about God is called preaching. Preaching is the single most important thing you will do as a pastor. If you do it effectively, you will shape minds, hearts, and congregations, sending them in directions they would not have gone had you not been there. If you do not do it effectively, you will waste the largest resource available to you.

The privilege of standing before a group of people Sunday after Sunday and reporting what you have found in Holy Writ is an opportunity beyond measure. They will hear you, gauge you, believe you, doubt you, form themselves in relation to you, ignore you, respond to you, follow you. You will, with your words, play a significant role in creating the people they become. Preaching is an enormously powerful element in a congregation's life, far more influential than we are sometimes aware. It shapes, molds, directs, calls, leads. Congregations will readily forgive their pastors for many other lacks if they are effective preachers. Congregations will struggle hard if their pastors are ineffective preachers, no matter what other talents they possess.

If you become a pastor, the greatest portion of your life will be devoted to preparation for preaching. It will start in seminary where you will learn biblical languages and content, biblical theology and interpretation. It will proceed into the whole of your life where in every book you read, in every newspaper you pick up, in every conversation you hold, in every event you experience, in everything you do, you will keep an inner ear alerted for moments useful for your preaching. It will carry forward into your work life, where the greatest portion of time you spend will be on sermon preparation: studying the Bible, reading about possibilities, formulating messages, arranging ideas, writing texts, and speaking what you have to say.

Many of us, when we are prospective or new pastors, get terrorized over preaching. Everything we have to say we put into the first sermon; how are we supposed to come up with the second? The relentlessness of each Sunday's arrival seems like the bane of life. Over and over, more than forty times a year, we are expected to stand before the same group of people and say something different and valuable. It can be downright frightening!

Then, if you have done your work, there comes a time when all that changes. It happens magically, almost without your being aware of it. If you have studied and taught the Bible, read a large variety of books, kept up with the newspaper, listened carefully to conversations, and paid attention to life around you, you will wake up one morning no longer wondering where the future sermons will come from. There will be so many you won't have time to preach them all. There won't be enough Sundays. You will find yourself having to choose *what needs to be preached most.* Your former great terror will become your great joy and opportunity.

Reading as prolifically as you can is a key. Stories, novels, news accounts, editorials, reports, analyses—they are all, with the possible exception of a few things like grocery store romance novels, valuable. But just as valuable will be your paying attention. Listening to what people say. Being attuned to what happens where you are. Picking up dynamics. Identifying meanings. Spotting universal connections. Everyday life provides more preaching matter than any of us will ever use. It is everywhere. The key is to learn to see it.

Whether praying about the people to God, preaching about God to the people, counseling, leading a community forward—words will be in the center of everything you do as a pastor. The adage says that "a picture is worth a thousand words." In some cases that may be true, but I'll take words.

Carefully chosen, artfully crafted words can be the most powerful, life-changing force in the universe.

If you believe in the power of words and if you can see yourself spending a major portion of your life devising them in the most effective and appropriate way, then, by all means, consider whether God is calling you to be a pastor.

Chapter 8

Conviction

A pastor needs to believe in something strongly, sincerely, deeply, and to spend his or her life acting on that belief. For example, a pastor may believe in working for the cause of world peace; believe in working to feed hungry children; believe in working to protect the environment against exploitation; believe in working for the reconciliation of enemies. The choices are many.

John Gardner, the founder of Common Cause, wrote: "Leadership is the process of persuasion . . . by which an individual . . . induces a group to pursue objectives held by the leader" (John W. Gardner, *On Leadership* [New York: The Free Press, a division of Macmillan, 1990], p. 1). Effective leadership begins with conviction!

It is very shallow for a pastor simply to be an amiable person whose greatest specialty is being nice. Being nice is good, but, by itself, it adds up to very little.

We pastors are tempted to settle for just being nice. Church congregations can be difficult places to work, being as there are so many different opinions around—on religion, on politics, on nearly everything. The pastor is not only highly visible—what she or he thinks becomes known by nearly everyone—but the pastor is also being paid by the gift dollars of the people who hold those many opinions.

One of the most tempting ways to survive is simply to be nice. Don't have opinions. Don't work from conviction. Just try to affirm everyone and make them like you.

This style creates innocuous sermons: God-is-nice theology and we-ought-to-be-nice-too ethics. It also creates bored congregations, and it creates pastors who don't know, down deep, why they are doing it.

"He's an awfully fine man." That can be a description of living death—also a description of disregard for the call of Jesus Christ.

This doesn't mean that pastors should be opinionated, quick to tell everyone else what is right. Few characteristics are more obnoxious.

It also doesn't mean that pastors should be single-issue people. God's justice, God's righteousness, God's love, God's promise cannot be reduced to a single issue.

But it does mean that the pastor will have a much clearer path by carrying a vision that quietly but relentlessly motivates her or his life.

When I was about twelve years old, I was sitting with my father one Sunday afternoon at a baseball park watching our Class C Carolina League Cardinals play a league opponent. It was a beautiful day, and the stands were full of mostly men and boys very much like us, neighbors from across our town. I knew these folks as kind, gentle, and friendly people.

In the middle of that game, I watched the first black baseball player I had ever seen walk onto the baseball field. Even though our town was 43 percent black, my middle class white world included virtually no one different from us.

I was shocked, stunned, deeply dismayed by the reaction that swept across the grandstand. Ugliness! Scorn! My fellow townspeople hurled hatred and derision at this young human being whose sole fault was his desire to play baseball in the most promising league he could attain. I had never seen that ugly side of my neighbors and friends before.

After a moment, my father, who sat quietly, looked at me very directly but also very caringly and said, "You are *never* to act like that!" My father was not a man of oft-expressed social conviction, but he did believe deeply in respecting all human beings. "You are *never* to act like that!" That moment told me that counteracting racial hatred was badly needed in our society. My father believed in it, and I determined that I would too.

It would be years in fully developing, but this conviction has run throughout my adult life. The dominant question facing this country from our beginning has been: Can diverse people who came here under vastly different circumstances, from vastly different cultures and languages, with vastly different skin colors form one nation indivisible with liberty and justice for all? Can the great divide of contempt and prejudice be overcome? I determined to make this a central theme of my life.

I have lost church members over it. In my first congregation, church attendance dropped from a steady thirty-seven to an equally steady twelve the weekend after our governing board debated whether African Americans would "be allowed" to attend worship.

I have also *gained* church members over it. Many people are attracted to a difficult but worthwhile moral challenge. They appreciate being asked to do things they believe matter.

But the main result is that, inside myself, I know who I am. The compass pointer isn't always waggling. The sails have a set bearing. I no longer wonder whether my life is invested in a worthwhile cause.

Recently, at a meeting of our denomination's national assembly held in our city, I sat for ninety minutes with a pastor friend comparing notes. "What are the most important things you have learned about preaching?" I asked him. My friend has been preaching for more than three decades.

"One thing above all else," he said. "Preach what you really believe! Preach your conviction! Preach your urgency! Those are the only sermons worth hearing. If *you* don't believe it, they won't either." He was entirely right!

Church committees who examine pastoral candidates would do well to ask, "What are your deepest convictions? Name the causes you really believe in."

As you determine whether God is calling you to be a pastor, identify a cause that motivates your life, an underlying commitment that propels you forward. Is it big enough? Is it larger than your own self-interest? Is it more than just you feeling wronged? Is it part of God's justice, of Christ's call? Are there slaves in Egypt who need to be set free? Will the cause be worth a lifetime of your devotion? If so, it may be that God is calling you to be a pastor.

Chapter 9

Create in Me a Clean Heart

A significant task of the pastor is to lead God's people in developing a capacity for healthy self-assessment, in the confession of sin.

A standard item in most Christian worship liturgy is the prayer of confession. In the prayer of confession, worshipers confess their own sinfulness, giving voice to the wrong they have committed and asking for both God's forgiveness and God's renewing power. We Christians believe that such self-critique is vitally necessary, that the life-renewal God offers is possible only if we have been honest in assessing the people we are. We cannot engage in a life-changing relationship with God based on pretense. God knows us fully and totally, and anything short of honest repentence is a sham.

We learn a great deal about confession of sin from Alcoholics Anonymous. A.A. asks—demands—that every member be brutally honest, beginning whatever statement he or she makes in a meeting with, "My name is . . . , and I am an alcoholic." What that statement means is: I have done wrong. I have made a mess of my life and other lives. I am addicted. I am not in control. I have hurt people. I can't solve my problem myself.

Alcoholism creates lying, bald-faced pretense, and no one gets healed with lies. The truth is necessary to become a new person. Honesty. Forthrightness. "My name is . . . , and I am an alcoholic."

I once took a church member to an addiction counselor to discuss my church member's problem. We sat down in the counselor's office. "Tell me your situation," he said.

My friend told his story. "I've been taking drinks since I was a teenager. A few times I have drunk too much, but not very often. I still drink some now, but I can control it. I would stop if it ever threatened to get the best of me. I've got a three-year-old son, and I'm not about to let my drinking destroy his future. Probably I sometimes overdo it, and that's why I agreed to come here today. I may need your help in not carrying it too far—knowing when to quit." This was the essence of a twenty-minute statement. The counselor listened intently.

When my friend paused, the counselor said, "Is that everything, or do you have more to tell?"

My church member thought for a moment but replied that he thought that was everything.

The counselor said one more time, "Are you sure?"

My church member said, "Yes."

At this point the counselor looked him straight in the eye with a piercing stare and said, "You don't really expect me to believe any of that shit, do you?"

My church member was stunned.

"What you've just told me is a monumental lie. You're lying to me because you're lying to yourself. I know, because I lived the same lie for fourteen years, and I recognize it when I see it. 'Basically, I can keep it under control'—that's the biggest crock I've ever heard. You can't keep alcohol under control; alcohol has you in its grip. It is strangling you, killing you.

"If you are willing to turn that lie of yours into the truth, to be honest with yourself and tell the story the way it really is—for the first time—then we will have a chance, a bare chance, of turning your life around and making you into a new person. But unless you want to stop living that lie, there's no chance. You will have to decide."

This story provides a stark version of the confession of sin. All of us live lies. All of us need to develop the capacity for healthy self-assessment. All of us need to confess before God the people we truly are. It is then that God offers us new life.

When Isaiah was in the Jerusalem temple one day—Isaiah, as a young man, apparently labored there—he saw a vision of God "high and lifted up." Isaiah's immediate response was, "Woe is me! I am lost, for I am a man of unclean lips, and I live among a people of unclean lips; yet my eyes have seen the King, the LORD of hosts" (Isa. 6:5). In the presence of The Holy, our first response needs to be confession, an honest portrayal of the people we are. God claims such people and grants new life.

The church joins Alcoholics Anonymous and a handful of other twelve-step programs in being the only organizations in our society whose members regularly confess their sin, who make confession a standard part their communal liturgy. Lots of organizations have communal liturgies. The Democratic Party, the Republican Party, the Veterans of Foreign Wars, the National Rifle Association, the Americans for Democratic Action, the Rotary Club, the Chamber of Commerce, the United States Congress—they all have standard words they say together when they meet. Not a single one includes the confession of sin. Can you imagine a Democratic or Republican National Convention that starts with an honest confession of sin? It would be considered ludicrous. And yet, can you imagine the redemptive effect on the nation if both Democrats and Republicans could engage in honest self-assessment rather than in the preening pretense that they are wonderful and marvelous and good and perfect in every way?

As I write this text, I am seated in a hotel room in Albuquerque, New Mexico. I'm here to lead a seminar. I arrived yesterday by plane from Kentucky, a seven-hour trip. With two bags in tow, I was checked in at the hotel check-in desk by a very efficient, very straightforward, very self-certain young woman who made it clear that things were to be done her way. She was running a production line, and all items on the conveyor belt were to behave as she wanted. She gave me two room cards in an envelope marked "613." I pulled my bags onto an elevator and headed upward. To my surprise, however, the cards did not open room 613, and in my fumbling to make it happen, the people who were already staying in room 613 came to the door to see what was going on.

I apologized, gathered everything and went back to the check-in counter. Waiting in what had by then become a longer line, I finally reached the young woman again.

"You mean you couldn't make the card open the door?" she said to me, implying that I must be one of those klutzes who has to be led every step by the hand. I had intruded into the order of her day, and she was going to make sure I knew how annoyed she was.

"The room has already been assigned," I said. "It is occupied by someone else."

She busied herself checking her computer screen and a drawer full of room cards. Then she disappeared into a back room. Returning a couple of minutes later, she thrust a new envelope with new cards at me, the envelope marked 1111.

"Here," she said, "see if you can make this one work."

The check-in clerk working at the next position apparently noticed what had happened. Stopping what she was doing, she addressed me: "Sir, we are sorry we made a mistake. I know it was inconvenient for you to take all your bags upstairs and then have to bring them down again. Please forgive us."

I smiled and said to her, "I appreciate that very much," which I did.

It was, of course, a small, trivial incident, totally inconsequential on the big radar screen. But it was a view into how hard many of us find it to admit that we do wrong. There seems to be a prevailing attitude today that to admit wrong is weakness. It indicates lack of self-esteem, lack of self-image—something you don't do if you aspire to be a successful person. Society's message is: we should cover over anything we do wrong, pretend it didn't happen, find someone else to blame. And, if there is absolutely no way to cover it over, then declare, "I just want to put this behind me and get on with my life," the final statement of denial.

We do this despite the fact that psychotherapists tell us that hundreds of thousands of people today are plagued by profound feelings of guilt, suspecting that there is something deeply wrong in us that has not been fixed. Psychotherapists' offices are filled with people who cannot and/or will not take responsibility for their own acts, people who are not able to engage in meaningful and redemptive self-assessment.

Adam, in Genesis 3, committed two sins. The first sin was disobeying God, eating fruit God had told him he must not eat, taking matters into his own hands and deciding for himself. That sin was bad enough. The second was worse: blaming his sin on Eve, saying to God, "The woman whom you gave to be with me, she gave me fruit from the tree, and I ate" (Gen. 3:12). He would not confess that it was he, Adam, who placed the fruit into his mouth and swallowed it. He would not own up to his own responsibility.

Among the most memorable words of the twentieth century was the comment, "Mistakes were made." These words were spoken by an American president who had engaged in presidential acts that were illegal and morally repugnant, a president who apparently came to view himself as above right and wrong and to believe that anything he thought necessary was right. "Mistakes were made." It was a classic moment in our culture's incapacity to accept responsibility, to confess sin. Other presidents after him would have the same problem.

Our society does a terrible job of confessing sin. An important task of the pastor is to lead a community and its people in learning healthy self-assessment; to demonstrate how, especially through a community's liturgy but also through individual practice, we are to own up to what we do.

The purpose is not to get people to wallow in their sinfulness. "Oh, I am such a bad person! I am inadequate! I can't do anything well enough! People don't like me because I am so much at fault! I'm terrible!" That is wallowing. There has been in our liturgy books a prayer of confession in which we call ourselves "filthy rags," ingrained with dirt, reprehensible throughout our being. This is not the kind of confession we want to teach.

The pastor walks a thin line. On the one hand, he or she needs to encourage people to be self-critical, to admit wrong, to accept responsibility in a society that often will not. On the other hand, he or she will need to move people toward "good guilt," not toward self-destructive guilt. If you become a pastor, you will need to spend your entire pastoral life figuring out how best to do that with a congregation of people.

Psalm 51 is the best prayer of confession I know of. The biblical superscription says that this is "a psalm of David, when the prophet Nathan came to him, after he had gone in to Bathsheba," giving David a great deal to confess. I don't necessarily recommend Nathan's method of direct confrontation of the king. It's a great way to get your head chopped off. But, as the presence of this psalm in the Bible implies, there are times when bold-faced audacity is what is needed.

"Have mercy on me, O God, according to your steadfast

love; according to your abundant mercy blot out my transgressions. Wash me thoroughly from my iniquity, and cleanse me from my sin. For I know my transgressions, and my sin is ever before me" (Ps. 51:1–3).

The person praying this psalm conveys no doubt whatsoever where the blame lies. This believer is accepting full responsibility. But the believer also knows that he or she is praying to a God who, in the words of Psalm 103, "is merciful and gracious, slow to anger and abounding in steadfast love" (Ps. 103:8), a God to whom confession makes a difference.

"Purge me with hyssop, and I shall be clean; wash me, and I shall be whiter than snow. Let me hear joy and gladness; let the bones that you have crushed rejoice. Hide your face from my sins, and blot out all my iniquities" (Ps. 51:7–9).

The psalmist begs God to set aside the sins committed, to grant forgiveness—knowing that this is God's nature, but still that the gift must be granted. Verses 7–9, of course, anticipate a redeemer capable of paying the full price.

"Create in me a clean heart, O God, and put a new and right spirit within me. Do not cast me away from your presence, and do not take your holy spirit from me. Restore to me the joy of your salvation, and sustain in me a willing spirit" (Ps. 51:10–12).

The purpose of confession is renewal! A clean heart. A new and right spirit. A redeemed person. That is the most fervant prayer of all.

Your task as a pastor will be to practice this healthy self-criticism yourself and to encourage your community to do the same.

This may well be the most countercultural thing you are called to do. The society around you will tell you it is a mistake, that you are weird. More than once I have had a church member say to me, "Can't we drop that prayer of confession from our worship service? Why tell people we are bad?

It's a downer, a negative attitude. I'd rather see us be positive, upbeat."

Our culture desperately needs the capacity for honest self-assessment, for true evaluation of our involvement in wrong, for the humility that comes from knowing that we are not perfect. A life of denial is empty pretense, a house built upon sand. A life of honesty is substance, a house built upon rock. If you are up to the quest for honesty both with yourself and with a community, consider whether God is calling you to be a pastor.

Chapter 10

God's Partiality

*T*his chapter is going to be different from the others. In the others I have deliberated with you the question posed in the title of the book, "Is It I, Lord?" In this chapter, I am going to preach to you. "If you become a pastor, then . . ." What follows is my reading of the Bible, my reading of the church, my reading of the society, my reading of pastoral leadership today.

If you become a pastor, I bid you to remember throughout your preparation and your work what I say to you here. The underlying purpose in the church is to create disciples and disciple communities of Jesus Christ, and this chapter is my commentary on discipleship.

All across the Bible, God exhibits a special partiality for obscure, powerless people—for the neglected, the disregarded, the unnoticed, the unimportant—or, to use the Bible's most frequent term, for "the poor, the widow, the orphan, and the slave." Typical ancient Middle Eastern gods were concerned with royalty, with kings, with powerful people, with decision makers, with the rich and elegant. The God of the Bible displays a radically different character. The God of the Bible is especially interested in the riffraff.

In Genesis 12, God appears to a migrant laborer (the literal meaning of the term "wandering Aramean" in Deut. 26:5), bidding him and his wife to become the father and mother of Israel.

In Exodus 3, God hears the prayers of a tiny slave nation, a nothing people within the great Egyptian domain, and God selects them as God's own special possession.

On Mount Sinai, God tells Moses that Israel's laws are to be tilted decisively toward protecting and caring for those with the least power to take care of themselves. "You shall not wrong or oppress a resident alien, for you were aliens in the land of Egypt. You shall not abuse any widow or orphan. If you do abuse them, when they cry out to me, I will surely heed their cry; my wrath will burn, and I will kill you with the sword, and your wives shall become widows and your children orphans" (Exod. 22:21–24; see also Exod. 22:25–27, Exod. 23:6–11, and many, many others).

God institutes the Sabbath in Israel primarily as a labor protection law, so that the weak and powerless will not be forced to work seven days a week:

> Observe the sabbath day and keep it holy, as the LORD your God commanded you. Six days you shall labor and do all your work. But the seventh day is a sabbath of the LORD your God; you shall not do any work—you, or your son or your daughter, or your male or female slave, or your ox or your donkey, or any of your livestock, or the resident alien in your towns, so that your male and female slave may rest as well as you. Remember that you were a slave in the land of Egypt, and the LORD your God brought you out from there with a mighty hand and an outstretched arm; therefore the LORD your God commanded you to keep the sabbath day. (Deut. 5:12–15)

Through Moses, God specifies clearly how Israel is to behave after it enters the promised land:

> If there is among you anyone in need, a member of your community in any of your towns within the land that the

LORD your God is giving you, do not be hard-hearted or tight-fisted toward your needy neighbor. You should rather open your hand, willingly lending enough to meet the need, whatever it may be. Be careful that you do not entertain a mean thought, thinking, "The seventh year, the year of remission, is near," and therefore view your needy neighbor with hostility and give nothing; your neighbor might cry to the LORD against you, and you would incur guilt. Give liberally and be ungrudging when you do so, for on this account the LORD your God will bless you in all your work and in all that you undertake. Since there will never cease to be some in need on the earth, I therefore command you, "Open your hand to the poor and needy neighbor in your land." (Deut. 15:7–11)

God tells Amos to preach mightily against a nation that lounges on fine beds, drinks wine in abundance, feasts on choice meat, massages itself with fine oils, and amuses itself with delicate music, but takes no note of its many brothers and sisters poor and destitute (Amos 6:4–7).

God lashes out against those who use their economic and political power to despoil their weaker neighbors in the courts of law (Amos 5:10–13).

God tells Isaiah to condemn and curse powerful Israelites who gobble up all the farmlands and leave no place for their poor brothers and sisters to grow their food (Isa. 5:8–10).

God declares God's intention to destroy the vineyard of Israel, a vineyard God prepared and planted with great care, because it produced wild grapes, sour grapes: "[God] expected justice, but saw bloodshed; righteousness, but heard a cry!" (Isa. 5:7).

In Psalm 72, God praises the king who "judges the people with righteousness, and the poor with justice" (v. 2), who "delivers the needy when they call, the poor and those who have no helper" (v. 12), who "has pity on the weak and the needy, and saves the lives of the needy" (v. 13).

Jesus, a young man, delivering his first sermon in his home synagogue in Nazareth, tells the assembled gathering:

> "The Spirit of the Lord is upon me,
>> because he has anointed me
>>> to bring good news to the poor.
>
> He has sent me to proclaim release to the captives
>> and recovery of sight to the blind,
>>> to let the oppressed go free,
>> to proclaim the year of the Lord's favor."
>
> Luke 4:18–19

Jesus tells of a highly prosperous man who "dressed in purple and fine linen and who feasted sumptuously every day." As he came and went from his finely appointed residence, the rich man never paid any attention to, never even saw, the "poor man named Lazarus" who lay at his gate begging for relief. (Luke 16:19–31; this story is a parable of what thousands of prosperous Americans do year in and year out in every modern city.)

Jesus says that in the final judgment, the sheep, who will inherit an eternal reward, will be those who provided food, drink, welcome, clothing, healing, and liberation to "the least of these my [brothers and sisters]." But that the goats, who will inherit eternal punishment, will be those who did not (Matt. 25:31-46 RSV).

Repeatedly, endlessly, the Bible testifies that God maintains very special ears for hearing the cries of little people, that God keeps special eyes on the plight of the least powerful, that God's heart identifies most warmly with the downcast and struggling, that God embodies a special partiality for "the poor, the widow, the orphan, and the slave." "Justice," a word that appears all over the Bible as something God mightily wants, is defined as repeating what God did with Israel in Egypt—hearing the pleas of small, weak, oppressed people and delivering them from oppression.

Now, with that picture of God provided by the Bible, what should be the priorities of the church I will lead in response to God's call? To build a nice worship sanctuary with comfortable pews and a good organ? To build ample classrooms for the entire Sunday school? To build a fellowship hall where the congregation can gather? To install air conditioning? To hold attractive worship services, traditional and contemporary, that will bring in numbers of new members? To preach sermons that will be both theologically and psychologically insightful, but not too challenging, and certainly not offensive? To teach Bible and modern theological thought? To develop a high quality church music program? To offer the best possible pastoral counseling for helping people patch their struggling marriages and survive their self-willed teenage children? To gather "people like us" into our congregation so that those who come here will find it "comfortable"?

All those activities may well be part of the picture. I have an organizational-specialist friend who talks about "the relational base necessary to create and sustain a strong organization," and the items listed above can be a significant part of that relational base.

But our theology, our belief about God, tells us to place one matter at the head of everything else we do, one item as the top priority of our church: God's partiality. God's tilt toward the disinherited. God's special concern for the poor, the widow, the orphan, and the slave.

There are churches all over this land whose dominant function is to keep the prosperous man in Jesus' parable carefully isolated from Lazarus languishing at his gate. Ecclesiastical life seems devoted to building walls to protect the righteous, on setting up spiritual islands where good people can enjoy one another, on proving Karl Marx right—that religion is the opiate of the people. Americans, with our frontier mentality, still believe that we can escape social problems by fleeing from them, and churches make a major contribution to the strategy.

The dominant spiritual question of our time is not: How am I going to relate to God? The dominant spiritual question is: How am I going to relate to my brothers and sisters? Am I going to treat them as God's treasured children, "the least of these my brothers and sisters," those granted dignity and worth by the hand of their Creator? Or am I going to treat them the way the world treats them—in hierarchies of importance, with some being highly valuable, some moderately valuable, and some not valuable at all?

Churches today are preoccupied with the development of spiritual disciplines: the institution of prayer, Bible reading, spiritual meditation, and self-reflection in people's lives. All of these are very good as long as they do not omit the spiritual discipline that needs to be, but seldom is, first in line—a redeeming relationship with the poorest among us, a serious response to God's partiality.

My worship is hollow, a charade, an exercise in futility, if my life during the week does not include reading for forty-five minutes with the child of a low-income family, or relating to ex-prisoners who are trying to put their lives back together, or working to build young lives through the community center next to a public housing project, or welcoming international refugees fleeing to this country because of the danger of violence in their own. If the prophet Amos is correct, and I firmly believe he is, God absolutely hates—despises!—the noise of our solemn assemblies and the melodies of our organs if they are not accompanied by justice rolling down like waters and righteousness like an ever-flowing stream (Amos 5:21–24).

God cringes at how easily we miss the point, at the magnitude of our blindness.

If you become a pastor, I bid you to determine that you will place God's partiality at the top of your pastoral agenda, that you will challenge every church you work in with this theology. Don't let people convince you that "we have enough needs right here in our own congregation that we shouldn't be trying to solve other people's problems. God wants us to take care of our own first." I have heard that claim many times, and it is a theological cop-out. If we are going to find God in our time, it will be through the faces, the voices, and the lives of struggling brothers and sisters, not through isolating spiritualism. We waste our devotion if we think otherwise.

I heard a powerful comment recently. Referring to Dr. Douglas Oldenburg, retired president of Columbia Theological Seminary in Atlanta, a member of the Atlanta city council is reported to have said, "When Dr. Oldenburg shows up at a city council meeting, you know that the poorest of our city have an eloquent voice." That is the reputation I wish for every church that professes to follow Jesus Christ.

Chapter 11

But, God . . . ?

*W*hoever wrote Exodus 3 did people like you and me a huge favor. Exodus 3 is the story of God's call to Moses—God's appearance in a burning bush in the Sinai desert to summon this shepherd, who was grazing his father-in-law's sheep— to return to Egypt and lead Israel to freedom. God's commission to Moses was formidable, a daunting challenge even to the most stout of heart. Egypt was enormously powerful, one of the truly great empires of the ancient Middle East. Egypt depended upon its slaves. Bricks were the building blocks of Egypt's grandiose building projects up and down the Nile River; and the brickmakers, though low on the socioeconomic scale, were critical to the final outcome. What God asked Moses to do would have been like telling the crew chief on a Chicago garbage collection route to appear before the mayor to announce that an unknown mystical Being wanted all the city's trash collectors to convene in Albuquerque for a month for no reason the mayor would ever understand. From the point of view of the Empire, God's call to Moses was absurd.

The great favor done for us by the writer of this story was the recording of Moses' resistance. Moses objects! Mightily! He cannot see himself as the person for this job! Moses pulls out all the stops in trying to talk God out of the appointment.

In Moses' objections—as so often happens in the Bible—we hear ourselves. Moses is a clear picture of our response to God's call.

God said to Moses, "The cry of the Israelites has now come to me; I have also seen how the Egyptians oppress them. So come, I will send you to Pharaoh to bring my people, the Israelites, out of Egypt" (Exod. 3:9–10).

But Moses replied to God, "Who am I that I should go to Pharaoh, and bring the Israelites out of Egypt?" (Exod. 3:11).

Here is our first objection: God, you've picked the wrong person! I'm nothing more than a shepherd trying to find enough grass for several dozen sheep to live on. I'm nothing but an engineer whose primary domain is differential equations and complex variables. I'm nothing but a history major who couldn't settle on anything else to study. I'm nothing but a Future Farmer of America whose biggest event each year is to display my sweet corn in the state fair. I'm nothing but a midcareer paper pusher whose life ranks at ten on the Dilbert scale. I'm nothing but a stay-at-home parent who has spent twenty years changing diapers, filling lunch boxes, and shuttling eager young wannabees to T-ball practice. I'm nothing but an everyday Mary or Joe who totally blends into the background and who, aside from some five-year-old refrigerator art, has never done anything to cause anyone to notice.

Most of all, I am not one of those preacher people—one of those religious types who conveys a pious air and wants to end every conversation with a word of prayer. One who disapproves of two-thirds of what other people think. One who radiates "you oughts." One who can stop a spirited conversation dead in its tracks simply by walking into a room. One whose mind seems always more on heaven than on earth. One who can't wait to die because life there is supposed to be so much better than life here. For God's sake, God, I am not one of those people. And, to be brutally honest, *I don't want to be one of those people!* Aren't you calling the wrong person?

What would my friends think? What would my family think? Wouldn't they stick me off in a "religious" corner and never relate to me in the same way again? Wouldn't I have to give up being who I really am? Wouldn't I have to stay out of pubs and dance with the shades down? I really don't think I'm the person for this job, God.

"Who am I that I should go to Pharaoh, and bring the Israelites out of Egypt?"

God's reply to Moses' question was, "I will be with you." That was the only answer for Moses' identity crisis, and it is the only answer for ours.

God said to Moses, "The cry of the Israelites has now come to me; I have also seen how the Egyptians oppress them. So come, I will send you to Pharaoh to bring my people, the Israelites, out of Egypt" (Exod. 3:9–10).

But Moses said to God, "If I come to the Israelites and say to them, 'The God of your ancestors has sent me to you,' and they ask me, 'What is his name?' what shall I say to them?" (Exod. 3:13).

Here is our second objection. What is your name, God? Who are you? Are you a pre-enlightenment apparition still hanging around to soothe the souls of those still mired in the seventeenth century? Are you the voice of my dead grandmother who always thought our family would be more secure if one of us became a pastor? Are you my unfulfilled need for personal companionship? Are you the soft, fuzzy pillow I need to jump into when things get hard and difficult? Are you the guilt my third-grade Sunday school teacher tried to implant in me? Are you my uncle who believes that the whole world is going to hell except for the few righteous like him? Are you real, or are you a product of my psychic need?

When I truly need you, how will I find you? Is there a sacred odor that will assure me you are there? A spiritual gesture? A prayer that will dependably invoke you? Is there a

place where I can always find you—perhaps in a quiet
meadow by a mountain stream or in a sunset of brilliant orange
hues? Is there music that will bring you to hand? Are there
words that will summon you, incantations that will call you
up? Tell me your name so that I will know how to locate you.

God spoke God's name to Moses. Names, in the ancient
world, were supposed to tell something about the person,
reveal a defining feature. But this name hid more than it
revealed: I Am. "Say to the Israelites, 'I AM sent me to you'"
(Exod. 3:14). What kind of name is I AM? What do we know
after we know it? Having sought clarity, Moses got mystery.
Having looked for a simple, accessible, manageable god who
would be present whenever Moses needed, Moses found
instead a fleeting encounter with One who was not to be at
Moses' ready disposal. Moses asked God's name; God gave
Moses an enigma.

You and I repeatedly seek to domesticate God—to put God
at our fingertips, only a prayer away. If we are going to be
called by God, we want it to be this kind of god. We want this
god to be always near—one we are sure to find whenever we
search; one whose name we know well.

This domesticated god is a god that will sell, a god that will
be popular across the culture, a god to be carried in one's
pocket, worn around one's neck, beckoned easily with no
more than a few words. This domesticated god will fill
churches, cram football stadiums, create movements, market
books, assure success. "Tell us your name, God, so that we
may always know how to find you."

The God of the Bible will not be domesticated. God comes
to us on God's terms, not ours; when God chooses, not when
we choose; in God's way, not our way. God reveals what God
reveals. For all the certainty we seek, we get mystery. God is
far more unavailable than available. God calls, but we can
never be absolutely certain where the call came from. We will
not ever fully know the name of the God of Moses.

God said to Moses, "The cry of the Israelites has now come to me; I have also seen how the Egyptians oppress them. So come, I will send you to Pharaoh to bring my people, the Israelites, out of Egypt" (Exod. 3:9–10).

Then Moses answered, "But suppose they do not believe me or listen to me, but say, "The LORD did not appear to you"" (Exod. 4:1).

This is our third objection. Suppose they take one look at me and scoff, "How could you possibly preach to us? How could a person who doesn't know anymore than you do . . . ?" What will I have to say to people who have lived far more life than I have? People who have experienced accomplishment and pain? People who know much more than I do about living in community? People who doubt education as much as they trust it? People who do not believe that a seminary degree is the magic key to anything? People who have survived the hard-knock exams and are still trucking forward? Why would they listen to me? Why would they think God has given me a word for them?

I remember vividly the first sermon I ever preached. It was to a new church development congregation that was worshiping in one tiny corner of a school auditorium. There were about fifteen people—I had met them for the first time the morning I arrived. One was an engineer, which gave me a small bit of confidence. Two others were teachers, one history, one economics—how little I knew in either field! One was a town alderman who was obviously accustomed to having his opinion matter. One was a doctor, confident in his value to life. Two were grandparents. I had had only three days' notice on this preaching invitation—I was filling in for someone at the last moment. I had crammed and toiled to write the best sermon I could, but I still didn't think it was very good. I was extremely nervous all the way through.

One man came to me when it was over, however, and smiled, "Hey, that was really good! You helped me! We appreciate your coming!" An angel from God. I will never forget him.

Church congregations are far more forgiving and appreciative than you and I think they are going to be. They are searching for a word, a learning, a perspective, and they come hoping that we, no matter who we are, can give it to them. The things they hear from our sermons are often going to be quite different from the things we intended anyway. "Suppose they do not believe me or listen to me, but say, 'The LORD did not appear to you.'" That worry is in our minds but not theirs. Convincing ourselves of that, however, can be hard!

God said to Moses, "The cry of the Israelites has now come to me; I have also seen how the Egyptians oppress them. So come, I will send you to Pharaoh to bring my people, the Israelites, out of Egypt" (Exod. 3:9-10).

But Moses said to the Lord, "O my Lord, I have never been eloquent, neither in the past nor even now that you have spoken to your servant; but I am slow of speech and slow of tongue" (Exod. 4:10).

This is our fourth objection. I can't talk well, God. I can never figure out the right thing to say, and the words never come! I freeze; I'm not interesting, much less compelling. What you need is a convincing person, someone magnetic, someone with a good speaking voice and a confident tone. There's no way I will ever be that person. I had an English teacher in high school who tried to make me a speaker and failed miserably. People yawn when I talk; they tune out and turn away. There's not a church in the world that needs the way I speak. I can't even tell a whole joke without people wondering how soon I will finish. "O my Lord, please send someone else!" (Exod. 4:13).

God replied to Moses, "Who gives speech to mortals? Who makes them mute or deaf, seeing or blind? Is it not I, the LORD? Now go, and I will be with your mouth and teach you what you are to speak" (Exod. 4:11–12).

In Moses' case, God appointed his brother, Aaron, who spoke "fluently" (Exodus 4:14), to go along as Moses' mouthpiece. God does not offer you and me such indulgence.

There are multiple other areas in which you and I are not ready when God calls. I don't know enough history to be a pastor. I don't know enough philosophy. I don't know enough literature. I don't know enough psychology. I don't know enough organizational leadership. "O my Lord, please send someone else! I'm not ready!" No matter who we are, we will feel this deep inside. God's reply is the same as it was to Moses: "GO!! I will be with you and will teach you." There will never be a time when we are "ready."

At the top of my church bulletin each Sunday, under the church's name, is the logo, "Ordinary people answering God's call." The term "ordinary people" is appropriate because that is whom God calls. God does not call the credentialed, those ready for the task. God selects shepherds who have been tending sheep in the desert, female judges holding court under a palm tree, fishermen hot and sweaty in their fishing boats, teenage girls frightened and shy, herdsmen and dressers of sycamore trees. In response to God's call, we pose a bundle of valid questions, good reasons why God should call someone else. Those doubts can nearly dominate our brains, making us hesitant even to consider God's call. God's reply is, "GO!! and I will be with you." That may not seem like a lot, but it is enough.

Chapter 12

Checklist

*A*s we move toward the end, I offer a checklist of criteria, a set of dos and don'ts by which I hope you will gauge yourself. First, the don'ts.

• Don't become a pastor if you are fundamentally angry at the world and are looking for a pulpit from which to declare your displeasure. Anger almost never makes good preaching, and it makes terrible pastoral leadership.

Yes, the God of the Bible sometimes gets angry. Once in a while, you and I are invited to get angry along with God—usually against cruel injustice done to powerless people. But anger as a fundamental personality style is self-defeating in the pastorate. Cynicism—subtle anger with a clever twist—is just as bad. And the declaration of yourself as a victim, in whose behalf all right-thinking people are supposed to join you in being angry at your oppressor, is the worst of all. Conservatives do it; liberals do it. It is equally wrong from both.

God is not dominantly angry. If you are, you will deliver the wrong message, and you will spend a career scattering emotional garbage everywhere you go. A good church staff can be completely wrecked by one anger-dominated person. If you are fundamentally angry, don't become a pastor.

• Don't become a pastor if you do not have thick skin, if you can't absorb barbs and criticism reasonably gracefully.

A pastor lives on public display. You will preach, lead worship, teach, pray, and direct meetings, all in public. The people with whom you do these things will have opinions. They will also be paying your salary. Most of them will be supportive and helpful, wanting to encourage you. A few will be critical, thinking they need to help you improve. And a smaller few will be totally insensitive, saying whatever they wish and having no regard for how it makes you feel.

No one likes to be criticized. It can hurt for hours or days. But if you have a particularly thin skin, if criticism sends you into an emotional spiral, if you become quickly reactive and have to defend yourself, if you invariably need to deflect blame onto others, if you can't listen to a critical remark, extract from it what you need to hear and silently move on, do not become a pastor.

One of my pastor predecessors used to say, "To be a pastor, you have to have elephant skin!" He was right.

• Do not become a pastor if you have an incurable tendency to drown everyone and every situation with words, if a chatter barrage is your natural mode. People don't want to be "talked at." They duck for cover, rightly. Your words will need to be restrained in number, carefully chosen and artfully crafted. Compulsive talkers are not what is needed.

• Do not become a pastor if you think it will make you a special authority on God's prescription for the world. If ordination will become your license to tell the people what they must believe and how they must act, stop right now. There are certain you-must, you-ought, you-should personalities who are attracted to the pastorate. To give this kind of personality the sanction of divine backing is a drastic mistake. Self-certain people who believe they have God on their side become tyrants.

One of the great scourges of Christianity in our time is the way the Bible's teachings and commandments are taken up by authoritarian personalities who use them as brick-bats for clobbering anyone with a different view. I once heard a sermon in which I counted seventy-two uses of "ought," "must," and "should." By the time it was over, the congregation felt thoroughly thrashed.

If you are an authoritarian person looking for divine sanction for spreading your moralistic certainties across the world, do not become a pastor. That's not what the church needs.

• Do not become a pastor because you have gone to a pastoral counselor for help with a personal problem, and you have found the help to be exhilarating and good, and you have said to yourself, "Hey, I could do that."

Pastoral counseling is wonderful. It can enliven hearts, renew relationships, and redeem lives. But it tricks some people into thinking that the ability to do it is the essence of being an effective pastor. It isn't.

In the past few decades, pastoral counseling has been an extremely popular element in seminary education. Scores of students have specialized in it. As a result, much good pastoral counseling now goes on in the church. We are prepared as never before to nurture the psychological and relational needs of the faithful. But there has also been a liability. Many pastors now think about their ministry primarily in therapeutic metaphors of brokenness and healing. Many sermons are little more than pastoral counseling from the pulpit. Many congregations see their primary mission as effective pastoral counseling. Some denominations appear on the verge of becoming large pastoral counseling networks.

An effective pastor is far more than a pastoral counselor. A faithful church is far more than a counseling center. It will be a mistake for you to become a pastor because you had a helpful pastoral counseling experience and have thought to yourself that you could provide the same thing.

• Do not become a pastor because your life has been exploited and traumatized and you are looking to be healed. Do not become a pastor because you think that in seminary and in the church you will find kind, understanding people who will help nurture you back to wholeness. Do not become a pastor because you have experienced rejection, and you look to the church as a place where that shouldn't happen.

All of us bear wounds. Healed or healing wounds can make us more effective pastors, people who know firsthand what others go through. But raw, open wounds are not a good basis for ministry.

Some seminary classes seem to have an overabundance of people who have been beaten up by life and who are having a very difficult struggle getting through it. I have enormous empathy for their effort, but seminary is the wrong track to be on.

The pastorate is not a place to get healed. You will not be an effective minister because you have a vivid picture of what is wrong. Bitter memories are no basis for ministry. If you are in serious need of repair, do not think of the pastorate as a place to find it.

• For God's sake, whatever you do, DO NOT BECOME A PASTOR if you are tempted to use your good looks, your charm, and your wit to manipulate vulnerable people into things neither of you should do. You will be around plenty of vulnerable people. Some will be attractive. Some will happily respond to cues you send. A few may even come searching for you.

I have known a handful of pastors like this, people who looked at life as an unrestricted sexual challenge. They are usually attractive, charming, and very effective in their work, people churches like. They practice their hidden malice once, twice, three times, as long as they can get away with it, never seeming to know that what they are doing is mightily harmful and profoundly wrong. They do not take seriously—perhaps they lack the moral capacity to take seriously—the damage they are waging.

DON'T! Don't get into the occupation if you lead this kind of destructive, self-serving life. Don't become a pastor if you believe in taking advantage of any desirable sexual opportunity that presents itself. You will create a terrible witness to the redeeming love of God in Jesus Christ, and you will leave a lifelong trail of unresolved wreckage and misery across the church.

• Do not become a pastor if you need a lot of money to be happy. A very few pastors make good money, but most don't.

• Do not become a pastor because you have failed in some other profession and you think this is something easier that you might be able to do. The pastorate may look soft from the outside, but it is anything but soft. It is demanding, sometimes demeaning. It takes talent, devotion, and hard work. You need to be a focused and disciplined person. A congregation is not a soft pillow for your failures. Pastors need to come from strength, not from weakness.

On the other hand . . .

• Do consider becoming a pastor if you find yourself intrigued by trying to read the minds of faithful people who lived two and three thousand years ago and discerning what they were saying to us about ourselves and God. You will need to spend significant amounts of your life doing this. You will learn Hebrew, Greek, Bible, theology, and a lot of history to help you along. You will struggle to bridge the multi-millennial gap between you and them. And you will need to develop a sixth sense for discerning what the ancients were saying through what they said, and for what it means now. It's a fascinating, intriguing, challenging endeavor! If it interests you, this may be part of God's call to you to be a pastor.

• Do consider becoming a pastor if you love creative

writing. Creative writing is at least a third of what I do. I would not want to be a pastor if I did not find great pleasure in it and have at least some resource for cultivating it.

• Do consider becoming a pastor if you like to read. Read everything! Theology, Bible, anthropology, sociology, physics, cosmology, history, *the New York Times,* the local newspaper, *National Geographic,* novels, biography, encyclopedias, the Internet—there is nothing you will read that won't help. Despite taking two speed-reading courses in seminary, I myself am a notoriously slow reader. But I get there, finally.

• Do consider becoming a pastor if you have a rich imagination and if you like to think beyond what has been. The church of the future will need to be significantly different from the church of the past. "Congregation" has pretty much meant one thing; it will need to mean new things. Sermon, worship, mission, Christian education, church music—they are all evolving. The paths are not charted. The best things to do have not yet become apparent. If imagination, thinking beyond inherited practices, is one of your strengths, that may be part of God's call to you to become a pastor.

• I have one other suggestion. If you become a pastor, select one thing you intend to excel at, one thing you want as your special talent. Develop it early on. Constantly nurture and practice it.

My choice was lay Bible teaching. Lay Bible study, for me, is the most effective way to intertwine the Bible with your life and mine. I love to sit with a group and talk about the meaning of biblical experience for us.

Select your focus, something you intend to do exceedingly well, and nurture it constantly.

Chapter 13

Seminary

I found seminary to be a very high-quality experience. It was strange, weird, quirky—yes—but fundamentally three years well spent. Seminary asks you to launch yourself into a superior education that is intended to last the rest of your life. You will learn history, two languages, Bible, theology, and some of the psychology of the human plight. You will be taught by some of the most persistent but caring professors you will ever work under, people who expect good things from you and who will do their best to help you accomplish them. Seminary will not be a huge, impersonal lecture hall.

There seems to be almost universal agreement that seminary is harder than college. Somewhere between five hundred and a thousand pages to be read in every course, tests, research papers, exegeses, theory, practice—you will know you have been to school.

But you are chasing the meaning of your existence, the purpose in why we are here, and the wisest way to spend our brief moment. That perspective gives to the whole a fundamental worthwhileness.

Seminary's main subject, theology, is a word derived from two Greek words, *theos* and *logos*.

Logos is the word from which English derives our word "logic." Literally translated "word" in the Bible, it means reasoning, considered thought, analysis. *Logos* is the best logical thinking we are able to do.

Theos, in the Bible, is translated "god." In reference to the God of Israel, its dominant meaning is Mystery. The Mostly Unknown. The One who cannot be possessed or comprehended. The One whose name is I AM, which tells very little. The One shrouded in smoke. The One whose thoughts are not our thoughts, and whose ways are far above our ways (Isa. 55:8–9).

The main thing you will study in seminary—theology—is literally the best reasoning we are able to do about a Mystery. All the logic we can apply to the finally Unknowable. All the rationality we can assemble in comprehending the Incomprehensible. That is seminary education.

There is one vital thing to remember as the education proceeds: the primary thing we are to do in the presence of Mystery is not to learn it but to stand in awe before it, to fall on our faces and worship, to experience the encounter. Seminaries sometimes forget that, but I can tell you that churches don't.

You need to go to seminary primarily to get a good education, not primarily to strengthen your faith. Your faith may be strengthened while you are there, but it may not. It may be beaten and battered, and at times you may wonder if you have any faith left. The main thing seminary will challenge you to do is learn. That will help *clarify* your faith, but to *live* faith is different.

To live faith is to invest your life in costly commitments that result from Christ's challenge and to trust God through those commitments. A layperson in my congregation once said, "Faith grows by risk, by placing yourself into situations where the only way you can survive is to depend on God." This woman regularly met refugee families at the airport and shepherded them through their initial time in this country. To live faith is to put yourself out on a limb for someone or something that needs you, and then to expect Christ to be there. People in seminary may or may not be effective in leading you that way.

Some wonderful people teach and study in seminaries. Some far less than wonderful people teach and study in seminaries. You will find humble servants and insufferable egos, self-giving wonders and self-serving jackasses, openminded people and rigid people, gracious souls and total jerks. Seminary is not what one student called "a land of spiritual giants." It is a land of essentially the same ordinary people you find anywhere else, except that they have joined in a special quest.

Seminaries are caught in the middle between being graduate schools and being vocational preparatory schools. On the one hand, they need to specialize in high-quality scholarship, creditable by the best graduate standards, acceptable to the academic guild. On the other hand, they need to prepare students to be pastors in churches, to teach them practicalities, to give them experience in congregational leadership. These two goals walk together uneasily. Most seminaries suffer a split personality because of it. Am I here to become the best pastor this school can make me, or am I here to prepare for further graduate study? Because professors are often leaders in the academic guild, seminaries threaten always to lose sight of their pastor-prep function.

The most critical time in your seminary education will be the first five years after you leave. Seminary is an introduction. You won't study anything fully. In your first five years after seminary, you will select what you want to carry further and set your pattern. It is a critical time; no one will be looking over your shoulder. Some church judicatories check up on the continuing education of their pastors, but most don't. You will have to decide as you walk out the commencement door that this, indeed, is just the beginning. There are few things more pathetic that a pastor of twenty-five years who essentially hasn't learned anything new since seminary.

I want to tell you four tales from my seminary life. Your stories will be different.

On the evening of my first day at seminary, there was a worship service in the chapel. A theologian from somewhere in the world was passing through town, and the community had gathered to hear him preach. The chapel was comfortably full of new students like me, of faculty, and of people from the town. I eased into the back pew.

During the second hymn, I noticed that in the row ahead of me was a woman literally writhing in prayer. She was tied in a devout knot, her hands glued together in petition. She would fall sideways onto the seat; she would drop to her knees on the floor; she would throw her arms upward in prayerful anguish.

I sat there watching. I had never seen anything quite like it before. The thought ran through my head, "Oh, my God, is seminary supposed to make me like this? If so, I have made a drastic mistake."

A couple of days later, I was emerging midmorning from the seminary library. Just outside the door, I found three of my fellow new students on their knees under a tree. This same woman had assembled them and was leading them in her prayerful writhing. She prayed for the souls of the lost; they whispered, "Amen." She asked God to feed the hungry; they whispered, "Amen." She prayed for the missionaries; they, increasingly inaudibly, said, "Amen."

Spotting me, she jumped to her feet and begged me to join them, taking my arm and urging me toward the huddle. I thanked her kindly but refused, wondering again, "What is going on here? Is she on the faculty? Is this something the seminary sponsors?"

I noted that this same woman ate lunch in the seminary dining hall, usually sitting at a table among faculty. She was, I soon learned, equally adept at English and French.

On the morning that Hebrew class began, she showed up

in the second row. With text and notebook in hand, she seemed prepared to study with the rest of us. She asked more than her share of questions and made about as many comments as the entire remainder of the class. This seemed to put the professor slightly on edge, but he proceeded.

On the third day, we were studying a fairly obscure Hebrew vowel pointing called the *dagesh lene,* a dot that can be attached to certain Hebrew consonants to give them a particular pronunciation. In the middle of the *dagesh lene,* this little woman rose to her feet and proclaimed to the entire class, "This is the fourth time I have taken beginning Hebrew. I have never understood the *dagesh lene.* I still don't. It takes me out of the class everytime." At which point she gathered her notes and marched out the door. We all looked at one another, stunned.

One student whispered, "I never imagined we would be saved by a *dagesh lene.*"

Another replied, "And apparently we aren't the first."

Our friend was a nearby neighborhood resident who apparently enacted this same script every year with the incoming class. It was the closest we came to hazing.

My first summer internship in seminary sent me to Covington, Virginia, a paper mill town in the mountains on the western edge of the state. Every summer, Covington sponsored a huge bloodmobile campaign designed to urge everyone in the community to help build up the area's blood supply. The centerpiece of the campaign was a parade through downtown on the morning of bloodmobile day. Each of the town's churches—in most cases the youth group— would build a float to enter in the parade.

My youth group decided on a Peanuts theme—Charlie Brown wasn't very old at that point. We built a float with a doghouse in the middle with Snoopy lying on top. Wrapped around Snoopy's arms were two thick blankets, and he was howling his head off in protest. Beside the doghouse stood Charlie Brown, Linus, Lucy, and others, each wearing an "I have donated" sticker, and saying, in letters posted above their heads, "But Snoopy, everybody's doing it!" The side of the float said, "Get off your doghouse and give to the Covington bloodmobile."

Two vehicles behind us was a float that still, in my book, holds the record for the worst theological slogan I have ever seen. In the middle of the float was a large wooden cross draped with black cloth. In large print on the sides was written, "He gave his blood for you; won't you give your blood for him?"

If you decide to become a pastor, please determine that you will employ theology more artfully than that.

One of my classmates in seminary was a young man I will call Roger. Roger had been born with severe cerebral palsy. He was extremely intelligent, but his body did not work in the normal way.

Roger had passed high school and college on sheer determination. His parents were both accomplished people, and he decided that he, regardless of his handicap, would leave his own mark. He wanted to become an editor, specifically of church educational curricula.

It took Roger a long time to read a book. He had to prop it at the right distance and turn pages by rubbing his thumb across them. But he had read plenty: novels, history, theology, education.

Roger had an electric typewriter with a metal cover over the keyboard that allowed him to swing his hand back and forth over it without touching the keys. Locating the desired key, he would push his index finger into that key slot in the metal cover. He had become really proficient with this process. Still, writing a paragraph took him about an hour.

Instead of walking, Roger staggered, appearing at all times

to be about to tip over. He was a husky fellow with muscles like rocks, for he used nearly all of them every time he took a step. If you were walking across the campus, heard frustrated sounds coming from the grass, and saw arms and legs flailing in the air, you knew that Roger had stumbled and needed help in getting up.

Almost every night, after the seminary library closed at ten o'clock, the downstairs door to our dorm would open. There would be a heavy shuffling across the hall floor, and then, amid anticipatory sounds of "ngf, aghh, mmphh," we would hear Roger's heavy shoes banging up the dormitory steps. He would stagger down the hall to our room and flop into a stuffed chair. Then we would laugh and cry with him through memories of the day.

In the spring of Roger's senior year, a small group of his classmates decided to take on Roger as their special project. They seemed to need to prove something, probably to themselves—that they really did have preacher capacity, the ability to make a difference in someone's life. As they faced the reality of heading out into the church, they needed a validation seminary had not provided. It was apparent early whose needs were primarily being addressed.

The group met with Roger one evening and told him that they wanted to deepen his faith, to make him a spiritually strong person, in the hope that God would heal his affliction. All that was necessary, they said, was for him to believe strongly enough. If he could strengthen his faith enough, God would heal him. This was most definitely not, I should comment, a theology taught at the seminary.

Roger was perplexed. He didn't really believe it. He knew better than to play this kind of game with God. He doubted that these students possessed any healing power. And yet, he had spent his life wishing, praying, to have a whole body. What if the students were right? What if they actually could make him new? And what if, in his skepticism, he turned them down? Would he miss his best opportunity?

Roger decided to try it. The students met with him each night for Bible reading and prayer. They earnestly asked God to increase Roger's faith. They held devotionals, they sang hymns, they meditated, they chanted, they lit candles. Nothing happened. They anointed him, washed his feet, burned incense, sent toward heaven every incantation they could devise. Nothing happened.

They increased their efforts, sixty minutes instead of forty-five. More praise. More fervor. More zeal. Nothing. More sincerity. More petitioning. More urging. Nothing.

They brought in a faith healer, a man known for success. They followed the faith healer's instructions. They read Bible passages as he directed. Prayed in his way. Laid on hands as he showed them. Believed as he exhorted them. Nothing.

Finally, after a month, the students gave up. They told Roger that he must not have enough faith, that they had tried everything and that his lack of faith was the only remaining explanation. They soon left campus for their new vocations, undoubtedly glad to leave behind this experience of frustration.

Roger was not at heart surprised. He had suspected the outcome all along, but he was deeply frustrated and worn out. He had poured himself into this effort, and it would take him several months to recover.

There were two tragedies. One was the scar left on Roger. He had had enough hard experiences in his life, and he didn't need this one. But the other was the greater tragedy—that the students had not been able to look at Roger and see faith—his step-by-step struggling forward, his determination against enormous odds, his trust, his devoted labor. Why, as they finished seminary and headed into pastoral careers, did they not have eyes to see? Jesus said, "The one who endures to the end will be saved" (Mark 13:13). That was a picture of Roger.

I have been privileged in my current pastorate to have several seminary professors and denominational executives in my congregation. To stand in the pulpit on Sunday morning and address these personalities is in no small measure intimidating. In many cases, they know a lot more about what I'm talking about than I do. Young associate pastors feel it far more. Preaching can be a profoundly daunting experience when you are addressing people who were your teachers only a few weeks ago. Given these dynamics, there is one story from seminary that has held great meaning for me. I was told this story by a classmate. Real or apocryphal, it leaves its mark.

A student at my seminary arose one Sunday morning and decided to attend worship at a church one block away. The preacher at this church was well known on campus for his flamboyant, straightforward, head-on approach both to ministry and to life. He was a kind, nice individual, a treasured pastor. But he minced few words, saying what he wanted to say very directly. We'll name him "Carlsworth."

In the congregation that morning was a seminary professor who had had years of experience as the pastor of a "prominent" congregation and was now spending his last decade teaching pastoral leadership. He was highly regarded, genuinely respected, almost regal in his bearing. He would later hold the highest elected office in his denomination. We will name him "Professor Jonathan."

The congregation worshiped. When the hour was over and the benediction spoken, Carlsworth stationed himself at the rear middle door, as was his custom, to greet departing worshipers. A line formed. The seminary student happened to be just behind Professor Jonathan.

Making it to Carlsworth, Professor Jonathan greeted him warmly and shook his hand. "Carlsworth, that was a fine sermon. I really appreciated it. You fed my soul this morning, and I thank you." But then, looking at Carlsworth a mite sternly, Professor Jonathan continued, "There was, however, one thing you said in point two that I think we ought to get together and discuss sometime. Nothing major, just a small point."

It was, of course, one of those moments of terror: "The seminary professor wants to correct my sermon. Oh, my gosh, what did I do wrong? I will not rest easily until I know!" The student cringed in empathy.

Carlsworth, however, looked Professor Jonathan straight in the eye and said without so much as a slight hesitation, "Jon, go to hell."

I cannot tell you how meaningful that story has been for me!

Chapter 14

Voices to Hear

*H*ow can you best discern whether God is calling you to be a pastor? What list of criteria should you consider? I have asked that question of a number of friends, and here, in distilled form, is the result. I present them not in order of importance; they are all important!

1. Pay attention to your heart. Do you believe, deep down, that God wants you to do this? Is it a compulsion, something you cannot escape? Does it repeat itself over time? Do you feel it strongly, not just in a vague glimmer? Does it come to you in many circumstances? Is the voice one you cannot quiet?

2. Pay attention to your teachers. Does your academic record suggest that a high-expectation graduate school is a good place for you, that a profession that asks continuing self-education and discipline is the right profession for you? You won't need absolutely top grades, but you will need pretty good ones. Can you learn languages? Literary interpretation? History? Philosophical thought? Theology? Writing? Speaking? Leadership? What does your school record say?

3. Pay attention to your friends. Get two or three people who know you well to give you honest evaluations. Use other people's eyes to see the things you cannot see about yourself. Call on people whose judgments you trust. Tell them you need them to speak honestly. Make a list of the areas you want them to

talk about: your leadership qualities, your ability to handle stress, your capacity for oral communication, your psychological makeup. Listen carefully to what they say, and take it seriously. Find outside-yourself help in assessing the person you really are.

4. Pay attention to your church. To the people of God. To those who have clear knowledge of what a pastor needs to be like. To pastors, to laypeople. To your church teachers. To youth advisers. To a seminary professor or two if you happen to know any. To the committee that will need to sponsor you in your preparation for the ministry. To the career evaluation testing that your church will probably ask you to undergo. One very sobering question can be: If you hear a call from God so strongly, how come no one else can hear it?

5. Pay attention to the Bible. Read it by yourself and with other people. Listen for what it says. Listen for what God says to you through it. Pay attention to the "feel" you get from immersing yourself in it. Especially as you read the call stories of others, ask if the same God is calling you. Sense whether you should spend your life treading the fields of the Bible's dynamics. Ask if this book can become the primary center by which you understand and interpret human experience.

6. Pay attention to your prayer. Ask. Seek a word from God. Implore. Beg. Incessantly, not meekly. Be like that widow who knocked on the judge's door asking justice (Luke 18:1–8). Knock repeatedly. Be obnoxious. Listen carefully. Expect God to reply. Expect to see a light that will direct your way.

We began this book with the fact that God calls people, calls us to leave our fishing nets, our country and our kindred and our parents' houses, our accustomed ways of life to follow God's bidding.

Biblical people were so familiar with this dynamic of God's calling that they developed a standard way of answering. It was a single word in Hebrew, transliterated "hin-nay-nie." When

God called to Moses in the burning bush, Moses replied, "hin-nay-nie." When God called Samuel, Isaiah, Mary, and the many others, they all replied, "hin-nay-nie."

"Hin-nay-nie:" here am I. Here am I, your servant. Here am I, at your bidding. Here am I, for you to do with as you please.

In 1981, Daniel L. Schutte published a hymn, "Here I Am, Lord," based upon that standard biblical response. Each line of the song asks, "Whom shall I send?" And the refrain responds, "Here I am, Lord. Is it I, Lord? I have heard you calling in the night. I will go, Lord, if you lead me. I will hold your people in my heart."

If you find yourself responding to those words, wanting to say, "I will go, Lord, if you lead me," wanting to spend your life holding God's people in your heart, then consider very seriously whether God is calling you to be a pastor.